PETER DOMINIC'S

Practical Cocktails

PETER DOMINIC'S

Practical Cocktails

JOHN DOXAT

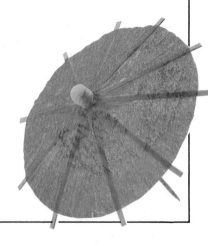

Quiller Press
London

First Published 1984 by
Quiller Press Ltd, 50 Albemarle Street,
London W1X 4BD

Designed by Tim McPhee
Design and Production in association with
Book Production Consultants, Cambridge
Typeset by Cambridge Photosetting Services
Printed and bound by
Blantyre Printing & Binding Co. Limited, Glasgow

PETER BRENNAN
Past President of the United Kingdom
Bartenders' Guild, mixed the cocktails in many
of the specially taken photographs.

A DEDICATION TOAST
to My Darling Wife

Diz

Who has drunk with me
through thick and thin.

Contents

Introduction — What it's all about
PAGE 8

1 Spirits
PAGE 12
Distilling 12
White Spirits 18
Gin 18
Vodka 22
White Rum 24
Tequila 25
Pastis & some others 28
Coloured Spirits 31
Scotch Whisky 31
American Whiskey 35
Canadian Whisky 35
Irish Whiskey 37
Other Whiskies 37
Brandy 39
Dark Rum 43
Calvados 44

2 Other Alcoholic Drinks
PAGE 46
Vermouth 46
Aperitifs 49
Liqueurs 52
Cider 60
Beer 60
Wine 60

3 Sundry Ingredients
PAGE 62

4 What is a Cocktail?
PAGE 66

5 Cocktail Equipment

PAGE 72

6 Shaking and Stirring

PAGE 79

7 Recipes

PAGE 82

Gin Cocktails 82
Vodka Cocktails 93
White Rum Cocktails 97
Tequila Cocktails 99

Scotch Whisky Cocktails 102
Other Whisk(e)y Cocktails 104
Brandy Cocktails 109
Dark Rum Cocktails 113
Cream Cocktails 116
Sundry Spirit Cocktails 120
Party Drinks 122
Hot Drinks 126
Non-Spirit Cocktails 129
Non-Alcoholic Drinks 130
Restorative Cocktails 133

8 Advanced Course

MORE EXOTIC COCKTAILS PAGE 135

9 Miscellaneous Matters

PAGE 141

10 Short Glossary of Drinking Terms

PAGE 145

D.I.Y. Personal Cocktails

PAGE 152

Acknowledgements

PAGE 156

Index

PAGE 157

Introduction – What it's all about

Obviously, this book is about drinks and drinking, about enjoying drinks – and mixing them. You would not have bought it unless you were interested in the subject. So we don't need to say too much about drink itself. However, there are matters that need reiterating, at a time when so many Prodnoses and killjoys are trying to tell us we are drinking too much, proclaim the virtues of abstinence, or even by law or taxation seek to introduce forms of Prohibition. History teaches us salutary lessons from the lasting harm that did to the U.S.A.

Our remote and uncouth ancestors enjoyed fermented liquors, for nature will provide alcohol spontaneously. Primitive people, when discovered by explorers, were almost invariably found to be making intoxicants from vegetables and fruits. The earliest civilisations relished wine and beer, and successive ones refined the processes until a dawning science invented distillation of potent spirits.

That early uses for improved alcoholic beverages were often medicinal is not without significance. Doctors may still prescribe alcohol for certain physical or psychological disorders. Perhaps the matter was put most succinctly a few years ago when a physician-psychiatrist cut through anti-alcohol waffling at a medical seminar by stating that alcohol is the simplest and safest of all tranquillisers.

That apart, alcohol has in all recorded times played a leading role in social life, in formal hospitality, simple entertainment, and, it may be noted, in major religious rituals. From tribal gatherings to diplomatic receptions, alcoholic drinks are an important element in bringing people into amicable relationship. In the home, a common custom in many lands is to welcome friend or stranger with the offer of a stimulating drink.

The dangers of excess no more need emphasising in regard to alcohol than they do in respect of eating, smoking, driving – or jogging. There have always been drunkards, gluttons, and, in modern times, crazy car-drivers and exercise fanatics. Drinking is an easy target for the intolerant. All excess is potentially harmful, if only to oneself: a man has killed himself by extreme addiction to healthful carrot juice. Excess – including zeal – is deplorable in any human activity.

We may envy abstainers their willpower; we may pity their deprivation (especially if the cause be physical); we certainly feel sorry for many of those whose national laws make possession of alcohol a grave crime. Sensible drinkers have no wish to impose their views. They simply want to be left in peace to enjoy their moderate and beneficial habits.

The New Cocktail Age

One of the most notable innovations on the social scene lately has been the revival of the habit of drinking cocktails and mixed drinks. Many people who have hitherto been accustomed to a straight Whisky-and-water or Gin-and-tonic are being much more venturesome. Perhaps on holiday they have tried and enjoyed more enterprising mixtures; maybe friends have

Cocktails accompanied Fashion Shows in the Roaring '20's.

introduced them to cocktails. The younger generation is avid for novelty, in drinking as in much else.

The first cocktail age was between about 1925 and 1935. It was a period of extravagance. In that earlier period to which we shall refer again, when strange mixtures proliferated, their use was confined to a tiny, if well-publicised, section of the populace, to the Smart Set and Bright Young Things.

The new cocktail vogue has a very different complexion. It is infinitely broader-based. Cocktails and their ancillary mixes are no longer confined to fashionable and expensive hotel bars or the houses of the rich. Many a public house makes a feature of cocktails and it is the norm rather than the exception for a home to provide guests with a choice of mixed drinks and to have a modest home bar or a cocktail cabinet. Off-licence stores stock a much wider range of drinks and sundry ingredients than ever before. There are exciting new drinks, such as Malibu and Bailey's. Cocktail equipment is readily available in a profusion of designs. Having enjoyed cocktails outside, it is natural for people to want to make them themselves.

There is no need to be the least fearful

that cocktail-making is a difficult thing to master. It is supremely simple, as we shall show. Several of the classic cocktails are, indeed, the simplest, which is probably why they have stood the test of time while most of the absurdly complicated concoctions of the former cocktail age are forgotten curiosities.

There are cocktails to suit every taste — even non-alcoholic ones. And an amusing aspect of cocktails is that they positively invite one to invent, to improvise, to impress one's own individuality on a new mix.

Know What You Drink

It must be admitted that the general knowledge about what they drink is not widespread amongst consumers: they usually have strong preferences, but not much information. It is unnecessary to learn the basic mechanics of an internal-combustion engine in order to like motoring, yet some practical knowledge can add to one's pleasure and confidence. By the same token, one can appreciate a sociable noggin without knowing anything about the products being imbibed. But it is an extension of enjoyment to understand whence they originated, something of how they are made.

And by increasing one's information, new prospects open. One's social life and home entertainment can assume more exciting dimensions — at no extra cost; possibly more economically.

So we included in this book a comprehensive review of the principal drinks of the western world. Some are very familiar, others less so, though we have avoided listing obscure liqueurs from European backwaters or peculiar brews of the South Pacific: to do so would be ostentatiously to display erudition at the expense of commonsense. We only mention wine in connection with its use in mixed drinks: it deserves separate treatment. On its own, wine is admirably covered in a companion volume to this, Anthony Hogg's *Peter Dominic's Practical Wine Guide* (Quiller Press, 1985).

We have endeavoured to produce a volume that, within a reasonable compass, will be a prime guide to the inexperienced whilst adding to the knowledge of the informed drinkers. We have left out technicalities: they may be sought in more austere reference volumes. We believe drinking deserves to be treated reasonably seriously, but totally without solemnity. Frivolity may occasionally be permitted.

Drinking should be fun: that's what it's all about.

Spirits

Distilled spirits fall into two broad categories: white spirits, and coloured spirits. All spirit is colourless when it leaves the still. Colour is achieved by maturing in wood or may be added: whisky, brandy and dark rum are usually colour-adjusted with a flavourless agent to ensure consistency of hue in a given brand.

There are three other broad divisions of spirits: those that have inherent natural flavour through their process of distillation (e.g. whisky and brandy); those in which flavour is induced (e.g. gin) and one important product (vodka) where the spirit is left in a 'neutral' condition.

Alcohol is a natural product. It is produced spontaneously by the interaction of yeast and sugar and is seen at its simplest in wine-making, when the yeast on the skins of the fruit meets the sugar in the juice as grapes are pressed. This is fermentation, which can, of course, be started artificially by introducing cultured yeast to a sweetened liquid.

Fermentation can only make a liquid bearing up to, at most, about 15 per cent alcohol. We do not know when man first tried to separate this alcohol from an alcohol-bearing fluid. Whoever it was certainly did not know that alcohol vapourises at 78.3°C and water at 100°C. Thus, if an alcoholic beverage be heated to above the first figure but below the second, the alcohol will become vapour whilst the water remains. If the alcoholic vapour is cooled before it dissipates in the air it becomes a concentrated alcohol – what we call

Stradamus: a distillery of 1660 ►

'Spirit'. In practice, using pot-stills, the earliest form (which remain an important aspect of distilling), the spirit from a first distillation will be fairly weak.

This is certainly what very early distillations were. It is thought that the Chinese were distilling a spirit from rice as long as three thousand years ago and that before A.D. spirits of sorts were made in Japan and India. It is generally believed the Moors brought to Europe the art of distilling (to make a spirituous base for perfume) when they occupied Spain. Certainly the word 'alcohol' is of Arabic origin – from *Al-Koh'l*, the cosmetic powder (*kohl*) which is a highly refined product – and became applied to spirit, which was a product of a refinement process.

Distillation, from wine, seems to have been fairly widely established in Europe about a thousand years ago, though virtually confined to the medical world, which effectively meant Monastic circles. Herbal spirits were found to have medicinal value, and for a very long time alcohol was, of course, the only known anaesthetic and, later, antiseptic. Spirit was known as *aqua vitae* (water of life), later translated as *eau de vie, usquebaugh*, etc.

Again it is a matter for conjecture, but at some stage it was discovered that a second distillation of the original spirit produced a much stronger, and also more palatable, spirit. With this, and the making of larger stills, the art of distilling left the alchemist's laboratory and became a practical commercial proposition: spirits entered social life. It is thought that over nine hundred years ago a complete concentration of alcohol from wine had been achieved in France; that is, a near 100 per cent spirit.

However, the first publication giving particulars of satisfactory distilling did not appear until the early 16th century. We may assume that decent spirits for general consumption were being produced around 1400. At that time, the light wine of French Aquitaine (see Cognac) was being weakly distilled ('low wines') to condense it for export and help its preservation. Yet the practice of second distillation – which eventually made good brandy possible – did not arrive in the region for another two centuries.

Another important factor was the discovery, probably by accident, that spirits, like wine, benefitted from being kept in cask. But not until our own times did maturing of pot-still spirits become usual and regulation by law did not become effective in Britain until the First World War. It was then decreed that no whisky could be sold that had not been matured at least three years. This had nothing to do with consumer protection – quite the opposite. It was directed at curtailing the mass appeal of cheap Scotch grain whisky which the remote powers at Westminster thought was affecting the munition-workers' efficiency. It did greatly reduce availability of grain whisky: the people simply switched to gin. At first thought to be a ruinous blow to Scotch, in the event compulsory maturing gave a great fillip to blended whisky.

Types of Still

The traditional still basically consists of a copper kettle. In this the alcohol-bearing wash is brought to the desired heat. Originally, the still sat directly on a fire. This made it difficult to control the precise

Interior of the Hennessy Distillery in Cognac.

temperature: if too hot, too much water is evaporated; too little heat, and the alcohol is insufficiently separated. Today, pot-stills are most usually heated by interior coils filled with steam: this gives easy control. The vapourised alcohol, containing some water, bears in it a degree of flavour from the wash; e.g. wine flavour in the instance of Cognac. This vapour rises and is trapped in condensers which cool it: it liquidises as distilled spirit. Pot-stills vary enormously in size. Those for Cognac are, by regulation, comparatively small; some employed to make Scotch malt whisky tower fifteen feet and contain thousands of gallons. There are various refinements to the pot-still, yet the principle on which it works is centuries old.

Apart from the desired flavours, some unwanted elements will remain in the pot-still products even when double-distilled. These can be removed by further re-distillation in a rectifying still but too much refinement by such means would destroy the character of the spirit. So, naturally flavoured spirits – notably whisky, brandy and rum – are matured in wood. No-one knows exactly why such spirits improve from lying in cask – but they do, very markedly.

Continuous Distillation

After a distillation has been made by pot-still, the still contains a useless water. This must be drained and the still cleaned before the next distillation can take place. This is not necessary in the process of continuous distillation, by which the highest proportion of the world's spirits are now produced.

In the early 19th century, a Scotch whisky distiller invented a form of continuous distillation. This was improved on by Aeneas Coffey, a retired excise Customs administrator, who patented his version in 1831. It is known as the Coffey (or Patent) still, and it was first operated in Dublin. It was soon used to increase the output of grain whisky in Scotland, was found useful in making unflavoured spirit for turning into gin in England and was soon being used in the West Indies.

A prime virtue of continuous distillation is that there is no interruption in production: distillation can go on until it is necessary to cease it for maintenance. The process is more complicated than that of the

Overleaf: Giant stills in a highland malt whisky distillery. ➤

No. 1 SPIRIT STILL

SPIRITS IN BRIEF

● Spirits are distilled from many types of fermented cereals and fruits. They are strong alcohols. The flavour may be natural or introduced after distillation. Liqueurs are not listed as spirits, despite their strength.

● For the most part, white spirits are highly purified during production: they do not normally require maturing. Virtually all coloured spirits are matured, sometimes for many years.

● Most spirits in Britain are sold at a strength of 40% alcohol (formerly given as 70 proof). Vodka is usually 37.5% alcohol: stronger (Smirnoff) ones are available.

● The contents of a standard spirit bottle is ¾-litre (75 cl), except that for brandy which is customarily 68 cl. Strength and contents must be displayed on all spirit labels.

● All distilled spirits are originally white (uncoloured). Colour may come from cask-maturing, or be partly (or wholly) artificial. In itself, colour has no bearing on strength or taste.

pot-still and we need not bother with technicalities. Continuous distillation gives precise control of the strength of spirit it makes, and this affects the amount of flavour. However, the main purpose of continuous distillation in modern terms is to produce huge quantities of highly rectified (very pure) unflavoured spirit, particularly from maize or molasses bases. These may become gin, vodka, grain whisky (when made and matured in Scotland) or 'neutral' spirit to fortify other drinks or, indeed, for use as industrial or surgical spirit. Huge amounts of poor, surplus wine are distilled into industrial alcohol as part of the French agricultural support projects.

We shall now turn our attention to individual spirits. The word 'spirits' is here used in the conventional meaning. Liqueurs are, for the most part, highly spirituous: however, it is customary to treat them separately.

Naturally, most attention is given to those spirits in general use. These have acquired fresh uses with the modern vogue for mixed drinks. Some less usual spirits are included to complete the picture.

GIN

The two principal white spirits are gin and vodka. In some countries – notably the U.S.A. – vodka has overtaken gin as the premier uncoloured alcohol base for cocktails. In Britain, though gin's leadership has been seriously challenged by the newer spirit, gin retains its traditional lead.

Gin is marginally stronger than most

vodkas. It also has decided character, which its devotees maintain is important to mixes which call for its use, from gin-and-tonic to a cocktail. Some will further aver that gin is a particularly healthy spirit since its flavour comes from the oil of juniper berries, a medicinal product of enormous antiquity. The word juniper derives from the Latin *juniperus* (youth-giving) which is a good justification for gin-drinkers' preference.

The other ingredients common to London Dry Gin are coriander, orris root, angelica and cassia bark. But each brand has its own formula, and there are minor taste differences. However, in mixed drinks these will not be very apparent.

The spirit from which gin is made is highly rectified grain or cane spirit. Rectification means complete purification by re-distillation. The resultant spirit is therefore as clean and flavourless as possible. Into this pure spirit the botanical ingredients – juniper, coriander etc. – are introduced by several processes; the technicalities are unimportant to the consumer.

A corner of the ingredients store at the distillery which produces the famous Bombay Gin.

Types of Gin

The gin in most universal use is the so-called London Dry type. In English-speaking and many other countries, the simple word gin refers, in practice, to this style. Why is it called London Dry? That is because London distillers historically dominated the British gin trade. About a century ago, in addition to their cordial gins – with a wide variety of flavours and often very sweet – they introduced 'unsweetened' gin, usually proclaiming that it contained absolutely no sugar. This was an altogether more delicate spirit than earlier gins, and it became favoured for such drinks as gin and Indian quinine water – our gin-and-tonic. When cocktails began to be popular, this unsweetened gin was found much more suitable than more pungent varieties. The term London Dry replaced 'unsweetened'.

All gin distilleries started making this lighter gin. Regardless of what country was involved, the description London Dry was used to indicate a type, not necessarily a place of origin. Today far more Dry gin is made outside London than in it. Some famous London gin distillers which were founded in London – notably Gilbey's – have found it convenient to move from the capital to facilitate expansion. English names dominate the international commerce in gin; the leading brands are very widely exported and also produced in many countries.

Flavoured gins have virtually disappeared. Sloe gin is produced commercially but is best concocted at home (see

Chapter 9). Likewise, orange and lemon gin are very rarely specified in recipes, and in very old mixes, which once called for scented Old Tom gin, Dry gin has long been substituted. Plymouth gin, a peculiarity of that port and formerly favoured by the Royal Navy for Pink gin (Chapter 9), exists as a brand-name but it has been revised to a much less aromatic, dry formula.

Dutch gin – Hollands, Genever, Geneva – retains the historic, heavy characteristics of the first gin ever distilled. Dutch gin has little place in the world of mixed drinks. It has declined in popularity, though remaining the traditional spirit of the Netherlands. However, Dutch distillers make a great deal of Dry gin. English gin is much counterfeited in some European countries frequented by tourists. Barmen, outside important hotels, often use cheap and unpleasant local 'gin'. Beware unknown 'London' type labels and misleading names. Travellers are best off buying imported English gin – or one made in the country by a familiar English company – and mixing drinks in their rooms.

Historical Note

The word 'gin' is in universal use. It is a corruption and contraction by the English of the Dutch geneva/genever/jenever, which derives from the French for juniper, genièvre. Like many famous spirits, gin started as a medicine: it was evolved in the mid-16th century at the university of Leyden in the Netherlands. The first commercial gin distillery was founded in Schiedam, now a suburb of Rotterdam, in 1575. Gin was introduced to England by

◄ Gilbey's Distillery by night.

returning servicemen and traders. It attracted some interest in ports and by mid-17th century its production in such cities as London, Plymouth and Bristol was well-established. After 1688, its popularity increased dramatically: one of the first Acts of the reign of William and Mary was to ban French brandy and encourage distilling in England. Gin consumption eventually became a serious social problem, particularly in London, owing to poor regulation of the distilling trade. Not until the third part of the 1700s did abuses of gin decline and its general quality improve. It was not considered a spirit for polite society until many years later: women were the first to appreciate its virtues. The advent of London Dry gin (see above) finally made gin acceptable at all social levels, and increasing use of mixed drinks ensured gin's enormous popularity.

VODKA

Vodka has enjoyed a phenomenal success worldwide since the late 1950s. It needs explaining that particularly in the context of cocktails and mixed drinks one does not think of traditional Polish, Russian or other vodkas, from historically vodka-drinking lands. There, vodka implies spirits both white and coloured, with a huge range of flavours – from pepper to chocolate. Though Poland, Finland and Sweden, for instance, do make entirely flavourless vodkas, and export them, they have little importance overseas. Flavoured vodkas, mostly drunk neat, can be excellent: they are mostly unsuitable for mixed drinks.

Vodka, as the term is understood by nearly all drinkers in Britain, the U.S.A., English-speaking countries generally, and many others, is white spirit completely lacking flavour. It gives alcoholic zing to whatever it is added, without affecting the taste of it. Such vodka is a pure alcohol which is further purified by filtration through fine charcoal. The quality stems from that of the original spirit and depends on the expertise of the distiller, whose reputation is the consumer's guarantee.

This, now universal, style of vodka has been described – to distinguish it firmly from traditional vodkas – as 'Anglo-American'. That is not an official designation, but it is as we shall see an apt one. Henceforward, take the word 'vodka', in all recipes, as indicating the Anglo-American style.

The advent of modern vodka, and its rise, can be traced to a single brand and one man. The story should interest any vodka-drinker: here it is in essence.

First, we must go back momentarily to Tsarist Russia. There, by 1912, the Smirnoffs, reputed the world's richest commercial family, produced a million bottles of vodka daily from a single factory on the outskirts of Moscow. In 1914, when the first World War broke out, vodka was banned. The subsequent Revolution spelled death, ruination and exile for the Smirnoffs. One member of the family set up in Paris in a small way. In 1934, a Ukrainian, who had connections with the old Smirnoff business, started an American branch of Smirnoff in the U.S.A. in Connecticut. It did not prosper.

Enter British-born John Martin, head of an old-established firm, Heublein, of Hart-

Some of the Smirnoff Vodka filtration columns.

ford, Conn. He met the Ukrainian, retained his services, and in 1939 Heublein's acquired the rights to Smirnoff. Sales of vodka in the U.S.A. were minute. Heublein's directors thought John Martin had made a mistake: after the war, John Martin was almost agreeing with them.

A Momentous Day

Then, one day in Los Angeles in 1947, John Martin, at a meeting with a bar-owning acquaintance, evolved the Moscow Mule, using a special copper mug made by a third friend. As things will in California, the new mix, with a mug gimmick, caught on with the smart showbiz set. Vodka first became a local speciality, and soon, with the Screwdriver cocktail and the Bloody Mary, began to sweep the nation. Vodka became a craze, but unlike many crazes, it survived to become an institution. People attributed all sorts of virtues to vodka – that it was healthier than other spirits, that you could drink more of it without side-effects, and so on. Fresh special vodka cocktails were invented. Heublein's was on its way from small, if respected, company to multi-national conglomerate; and Smirnoff was on its way to world fame and to become leader of a new pattern in spirit-drinking.

The first country to take up Smirnoff outside the United States was the U.K. It seemed most unlikely that Britain would take to this novelty, but Gilbey's, the celebrated gin distillers, had the foresight to believe that vodka might prove as popular as it was becoming across the Atlantic: if it did, it would compete with gin. In that case, they wanted to be in a strong position. In the 1950s, Gilbey's obtained the British rights to produce Smirnoff and launched it on an apathetic public. It took several years for vodka to gain any real hold in Britain: oddly, the vogue for it started in Scotland. But when vodka did catch on, aided by brilliant advertising, its popularity spread as fast as it had in the U.S.A. Other vodka brands appeared: Smirnoff was already far ahead of them. Gilbey's had been as prescient as John Martin. Smirnoff is produced in many countries, and sold globally. Smirnoff's international success has encouraged scores of vodka brands: none has achieved similar universal acclaim.

The bright, clear vodka with which we mix pleasing drinks today is a far cry from the *zhizennia voda* (water of life), vodka's ancestor, the herbal spirit by legend originating nine hundred years ago in a monastery of old Muscovy.

WHITE RUM

White rum is so different in flavour to traditional dark rum that it may, for purposes of mixing drinks, be treated as a separate commodity. Recent times have seen a dramatic rise in its popularity, in tune with the fashion for light drinks. It is an admirable cocktail spirit.

A few words about the nature of rum are in order. Under British law, to be called 'rum', a spirit must be distilled from cane sugar in a cane sugar-producing country. Britain is not a cane sugar producing country. So, although it produces a lot of sugar, from beet, neither that sugar, nor imported molasses, may be used as the base for a spirit to be called rum. By far the most important rum-producing areas are the West Indies and the Caribbean, including the adjacent South American mainland.

But cane sugar countries the world over have some form of rum. The single largest producer of rum is Puerto Rico. In earlier times, different areas had their own very distinctive types – Cuban, light; Demerara (Guyana), dark; Jamaica, pungent, for instance. Nowadays, most producers make various styles to compete in a very important spirit market: regional specialisation has lost significance.

As a word, rum's origin is not decided. It may stem from the Spanish *ron* – quite likely as old Spain's colonies were very early distillers from sugar; or from the Latin *saccahrum* (sugar), or even from 'rumbustion', which was formerly used to describe strong drink.

Rum is made by fermenting the juice of the sugar cane or from molasses, which is a very sweet by-product in refining cane sugar. This fermentation, which is very fierce in a tropical climate, produces an alcohol-bearing liquid. From this is distilled a strong spirit. At one time, traditional pot-stills were used: these have been mostly replaced by modern continuous stills which can cope with the huge quantities demanded by commerce.

Continuous stills give a high degree of control as to how much flavour from the molasses or sugar is carried into the rum. Usually today, the rum is brought off the still with a minimum of flavour. It is now, in effect, white rum and perfectly ready for drinking, though under British law it must be matured in wood for twelve months: some are longer mellowed in cask. (How dark rums are made is dealt with under Coloured Spirits.) If the rum picks up more colour from the maturing process than is cared for by the brand-owner, it will be de-coloured to be an absolutely clear spirit. Some white rum is so light in taste that, in a mixed drink, it is virtually indistinguishable from vodka, which may also be a cane spirit: others have more decided character. There is a wide choice.

TEQUILA

Up until a few years ago, even in the United States – except in border regions – few people outside Mexico had ever drunk that country's national spirit, tequila. It had an, often justified, reputation for extreme harshness. The local manner of taking it – neat, with salt and acidic fresh lime – was a custom that amused tourists but suggested that tequila needed powerful counter-balances. A few sophisticates were conversant with the Margarita cocktail, but until the middle 1960s tequila did not loom large in the catholic and adventurous drinking patterns of American social life.

The cactus-like plants from which Tequila is eventually distilled.

The first stage in the production of white rum is to bring large quantities of sugar cane to the processing plants.

Things are very different today. Tequila has become a major and fashionable spirit throughout the U.S.A. and is engaging an increasing interest amongst young and venturesome persons in Europe and beyond.

Tequila takes its name from an early Spanish settlement in Mexico, where they established a distillery to make spirit from the native alcoholic brew. The name was later incorporated in the horticultural title for the plants from which the best tequila is produced, the *tequilana weber*. They are cabbage-like succulents producing single large fruits: these are cooked, the juice is extracted, and is fermented. This very highly flavoured fermentation is twice distilled to produce tequila.

The *tequilana* takes a dozen years to reach harvesting condition. In view of the vastly increased demand, the Mexican government has allowed pure tequila to be diluted with other spirit. Stringent quality controls are exercised over exported tequila, and, in practice, this dilution may have helped Tequila's popularity by modifying its traditionally intense flavour. Standard export quality Tequila is matured in wood for from three to five years. (Older tequila *maduro* is aged for up to ten years.) Modern tequila is a smooth spirit, with much more tang than vodka or gin, a sharpness which can prove attractive in cocktails. Tequila's taste is quite unlike that of any other spirit. It is a type of drink you either like or find intolerable; however, outside Mexico, its sole producer, it is very rarely drunk straight.

Over twenty million bottles of tequila go into American mixed drinks annually – so tequila must have something.

PASTIS and Some Others

In practice, the word 'pastis' is used to describe a wide range of alcohols in which the dominant flavour is aniseed. They may vary as to additional herbal ingredients: pastis usually contains liquorice as well as aniseed.

By far the best-known are the French Ricard and Pernod, now under the same ownership though in fierce competition. Purists contend that Pernod is just Pernod, and not a true pastis: no-one denies Ricard is pastis, from Marseilles. Pastis occurs in numerous cocktail recipes, usually in small amounts (a teaspoon or less), for the taste is highly pervasive. (There is also slightly different Pernod pastis '51, a reference to its year of introduction and also its recommended dilution, 5–1, when diluted with iced water – or, in Britain, often with bitter-lemon or fizzy lemonade.) The standard Pernod and Ricard are most usually employed in mixed drinks. In recipes, we specify Pernod but by all means use Ricard or any other good brand. Occasionally, but not in this book, you will find absinthe mentioned in a recipe: this is ridiculous. Absinthe has long been banned in many countries. Pastis was evolved as a substitute: it has essentially the same taste as absinthe, without allegedly harmful and addictive ingredients.

Somewhat similar to French pastis – but not always of equal quality – are the Ouzo of Greece and Spanish Ojen (*O-hen*). Aniseed is also the most popular main flavouring for Arrack (Raki, Rakia, Arak) made, from the Levant to the Orient, from

The versatility of Pernod . . . ➤

WHITE SPIRITS IN BRIEF

There is more detail for those who wish it, but here are the basic facts about the principal ones. Other spirits are also covered in the main section.

Gin is a pure spirit flavoured with juniper and other ingredients. By far the most popular type internationally is London Dry. Dutch gin is more pungent and not much used for mixed drinks.

Vodka as generally understood in the West is a totally unflavoured spirit, ideal for cocktails and other mixes. More traditional vodka is usually (but not always) flavoured in various way.

White Rum is a very mildly flavoured distillation from molasses; it mixes well.

Pernod, Ricard, etc. are pastis-style spirits fairly heavily flavoured with aniseed and other herbal ingredients.

Aquavit covers a very broad spectrum of Scandinavian spirits, the main flavouring being caraway.

spirits based on anything from grapes to dates. Fine Arrack from Indonesia gives the kick to Swedish Punsch, usually described as a liqueur.

Cautionary Note

When employing Pernod, and like products, in a mixed drink, try not to employ a measure you will be using for other drinks. Even after washing, the powerful *anis* taste may linger. While aniseed is one of the most popular of all flavours, it is unpleasant if it accidently contaminates, say, a measure also used for a whisky. Further, a number of people intensely dislike even a hint of aniseed.

Aquavit

Though aquavit (akavit) plays a small role in mixed drinks the generic term covers too wide a range of Scandinavian spirits, including the Germanic Schnapps, for this group to be ignored. Aquavits are variously flavoured, usually white, alcohols that are mainly drunk chilled and straight, frequently accompanied by savoury titbits or a beer chaser. The usual base materials are potatoes or cereals. They are highly rectified spirits. The flavouring is infused into them: caraway is a favourite. Schnapps is a far-ranging word – it even describes such spirits as whisky – and includes the comparatively low-strength Kornbrandtweins that are very popular in Germany. These have sundry flavourings, *apfelkorn* (apple) being an attractive example.

'White Alcohols'

A large group of white spirits, known in France as *alcools blancs*, would in Britain be classed colloquially amongst 'fruit brandies'. The French are extremely fond of these: there is a considerable variety of them. They should not be confused with cherry brandy, apricot brandy and the like, which are brandy into which fruit flavour (and usually sugar) have been introduced. *Alcools blancs* are distilled from the fruit itself – almost any fruit except grape. They are not sweetened.

There are two processes. The first is for a mash of fruit (or just the juice) to be fermented and a distillation made from this, whereby the essence of the fruit is carried into the alcohol. The other method is to steep the fruit in alcohol and then re-distil this naturally flavoured spirit. Both systems produce excellent *eau de vie.*

Eau de vie is French for any spirit that may be imbibed. Thus, a distillation from strawberries is, technically, *eau de vie de fraise.* However, it is most unlikely that the words *eau de vie* will appear on the label of a reputable brand. Most likely, it will simply state *Fraise* or *Framboise* (raspberry) or the name of some other fruit. In practice, the term *eau de vie* tends to be employed, usually conversationally, in connection with low quality spirits.

The best-known of the *alcools blancs* is certainly Kirsch, double-distilled from cherry juice, often with the crushed stones involved to give an agreeably sharp after-taste. These true 'fruit brandies' are naturally dry. A virtue claimed for them is that, unlike most spirits, they may improve with bottle age.

Poire William is an admired 'fruit brandy', from the juice of the William's pear. For expensive varieties, a pear is grown in a bottle, which is subsequently filled with 'pear brandy'. With this gimmick you get rather less spirit for your money.

Ordinary 'pear brandy' is simply described as *eau de vie de poire* (pear spirit).

Other fairly well-known 'fruit brandies' are the Balkan Slivovitz (from plums) and the Peach (*osze barrack*) and Apricot (*palinka barrack*) distillations associated particularly with Hungary.

White spirits from fruit are common throughout Europe. They are of more interest to the holiday-maker than the domestic drinker.

WHISKY

Whisky is a far-ranging description. Whilst to some it may instinctively mean Scotch – or Canadian, or Bourbon, or Irish – whisky itself is not a protected description. Whisky is made all over the world: even Communist China produces a 'whisky'. Only when the word 'whisky' is preceded by a geographical prefix does it take on particular significance. The spelling of whisk(e)y in alternative ways is a convention of comparatively recent origin.

Scotch Whisky

At the heart of Scotch whisky is malt. Malt whisky is made only from barley. The initial process is analogous to the brewing of beer. The barley is moistened and produces a short sprout about the length of a thumbnail. The water is of the utmost importance: Scottish distilleries are sited, often remotely, in close proximity to pure, natural water. The germination is stopped by drying the barley, the heat being permeated with peak smoke. The sprouts are removed (they are good cattle feed) and the malted barley is milled coarsely.

Hot water – from the same pure source as started the germination – is added. This makes a mash from which comes a sweet liquid, the wort. This is drawn off. The residual barley solids (draff) are another splendid fodder. The cooled wort goes into huge vessels called wash-backs. Yeast is added and fermentation commences.

When fermentation is completed, a type of 'beer' results. This is transferred to a big pot-still, the wash still. The distillation from this is a weak and rather impure spirit, called by the ancient name of 'low wines'. These are pumped into a second pot-still (the spirit still). From this comes a concentration of the spirit – Scotch malt whisky. But not yet legally Scotch whisky. It goes into casks, where it will stay for a minimum of three years, and maybe up to twenty. This maturation is vital. Not only does it mellow the whisky, dissipating many unwanted elements (congenerics) inherent in any pot-stilled spirit; the Scottish air in which it rests permeates through the wood and contributes, as has the special water, to the character of the whisky. The charred oak of the casks will give natural colour to the spirit. The timber of the casks is soaked in sherry – at one time old sherry casks were used – and this is another distinctive aspect of Scotch whisky production.

There are well over a hundred malt whisky distilleries in Scotland, varying greatly in size, each having its own particular style. Yet a strange fact is that although the world reputation of Scotch, its ancient inception and immense later success, have depended solely on malt whisky, straight

◄ **The typically romantic setting of a highland Scotch whisky distillery.**

malt represents only a tiny fraction of the Scotch sold internationally directly for consumption.

Malt whisky has a wonderful pungency, varying from mild to powerful, which has attraction only for a minority of whisky drinkers. It is taken neat or only with a little pure water. Sparkling water will enhance the flavour: ice will harm it. Malt whisky is not used in mixed drinks: that would be a form of desecration. In Scotland itself, no more than 5 per cent of whisky consumed is straight malt. Nearly all malt goes into blended whisky: that is the style on which Scotch whisky's universal appeal is firmly founded.

We must delve briefly into history.

The Triumph of Blends

Usque-baugh (water of life) was first mentioned in Scottish chronicles, in a form recognisable as malt whisky, in 1494. Distilling in Scotland is certainly older than that. It was for centuries an adjunct to small-scale farming, a way of using spoiled or surplus barley – pretty rough stuff. As early as 1644, efforts were made to tax whisky. More serious attempts were made after the final subjugation of the Highlands in 1745. They were ineffective: illicit distilling flourished until the 1820s, when the trade began to be regulated satisfactorily. Quality improved. But for some time, Scotch whisky remained little known in England except along the Borders.

In the 1830s, a new type of still, the Coffey or continuous still (see Distillation) was perfected in Scotland. This made it possible to produce a new style of whisky, grain whisky. It contained little barley; the

An illicit Scotch whisky distillery in a bygone age.

mash was mostly maize, not peat-dried. Grain whisky was much lighter than malt and gained a considerable hold on the market.

In the 1860s, an enterprising distiller hit on the notion of combining the full character of malt with the blandness of grain whisky. Thus was blended whisky invented. For a long time, the malt and grain whisky interests fought a battle for supremacy. In the event, neither won, for it was blend that triumphed. Its invention coincided with the lifting of onerous restrictions on the sending of Scotch whisky to England in bottle. Blended whisky was found to be very much to the English taste. A few years later, the phylloxera – the scourge which temporarily destroyed continental vineyards – made French brandy rare and expensive. Scotch largely replaced it, and also eventually demoted to a poor second place Irish whiskey, which had previously been the only type commonly found in England. Grain whisky continued to be fairly popular until the First World War. It then declined to its present virtual non-existence so far as the consumer is concerned. It is produced in Scot-

Whisky at its early stage leaving the stills.

land in enormous quantities, for use in blended whisky. It, too, must be matured for at least three years before being mixed with Malts. If an age is stated on the label of a bottle of Scotch, it is that of the youngest whisky in a blend. If a brand of Scotch whisky does not specify it is a malt, it is a blend: some blends contain as many as sixty different whiskies. Blended Scotch is the spirit base for a great many splendid mixed drinks. This is sometimes deplored by connoisseurs of whisky: they say Scotch is too good to have other flavours added to it. Nonsense: most favoured additive in Scotland for the country's great national spirit is fizzy lemonade.

American Whiskey

When we talk of American whiskey, we almost invariably mean Bourbon. There are, in fact, thirty definitions in law of American whiskey, from the finest aged Bourbon to whiskeys which contain no more than 20 per cent true whiskey, the rest being simply plain spirit.

Bourbon, a name protected by Act of Congress, is made from a mash containing

Quality control of grains at the Jack Daniels distillery in Tennessee.

at least 51 per cent maize (corn in the U.S.A.). The strict regulations on production and prescribed methods of maturing involve bourbon becoming a rather highly flavoured whiskey. It has its devotees throughout the world, but outside the U.S.A. is more likely to be taken in the famous mixed drinks associated with it than any other way. Bourbon is a product of high quality. There are three types. Straight Bourbon, from a single distillery; straight blended Bourbon, all Bourbon but from different distilleries; and blended Bourbon (not much exported) which need

be only fifty per cent Bourbon: if more diluted than that the word Bourbon is prohibited.

Another American whiskey of some significance abroad is rye; made from at least 51 per cent rye. This is lighter (some might also say harsher) than Bourbon and does not have the same status. Just as Bourbon is used colloquially – but incorrectly – to describe American whiskey in general, so rye is often – again improperly – employed in reference to American and Canadian whisky.

The third distinctive American whiskey

of merit is Sour Mash. Tennessee Sour Mash is particularly distinguished, and costly – it is not for cocktails. Tennessee whiskey contains malted barley, maize and rye, and the best is charcoal-filtered. It is of pronounced flavour. 'Sour mash' is a fermentation detail involving the use of some residue from earlier fermentations.

Canadian Whisky

Canadian whisky may owe its widespread distribution around the world to being a spirit combining excellent characteristics of Scotch and Bourbon and rye. The principal grain used is maize, with a little rye and a proportion of malted barley. Produced mainly by continuous distillation, Canadian whisky is on the light side, an excellent mixer spirit and also much drunk with ginger ale. It is almost all a blend of several distillations. Canadian whisky may be satisfactorily substituted for American whiskey in mixed drinks.

Irish Whiskey

Irish is undoubtedly the oldest whiskey: Irish monks introduced distilling into Scotland. The distillery at Bushmills, in Ulster, must be the world's senior distilling foundation remaining in production. It makes a distinctive whiskey, of which the premium variety, Bushmill's Black, is the best: not for mixing, but rather to be savoured neat as an after-dinner digestive.

In the Irish Republic there was once a proliferation of distilleries, as still pertains with Scottish malt distilleries. The number in Ireland declined, partly through the irrisistible invasion by Scotch whisky. Eventually only three important distilling companies remained: in 1966, they amalgamated. A variety of brand-names survived.

Irish whiskey alone contains oats. The other cereals in the mash are barley (malted and unmalted), and some rye and wheat. The whiskey comes, uniquely, from a treble distillation, and by tradition it is matured for seven years. Irish whiskey is consequently always smooth: the flavour is broadly fuller than blended Scotch. A fair number of modern cocktails have been invented for Irish whiskey, but its principal international fame lies, perhaps, in Irish Coffee.

One can scarcely write about Irish whiskey without mentioning Potheen, the famous illegal distillation which remains a widespread minor cottage industry. (The word is spelt in sundry ways, and is pronounced something like 'poyschyn'.) Well-made Potheen tastes like a very light, white whiskey with no discernible origin – quite pleasing. The trouble is that, having no maturity, it may produce near disastrous 'hangovers'.

Other Whiskies

This is not really the book in which to go into such spirits as Japanese whisky. However, in terms of world sales, it is such an enormous product, that to write of whisky and ignore it is to invite criticism. Japanese whisky competes, in the vast Oriental market, very strongly with Scotch and, for that matter, with Bourbon and Canadian. Japan used to imitate Scotch, down to (often hilarious) mock-Scottish labels. The joking stage has passed. Though buying much Malt from Scotland for blending, Japanese whisky has established its own identity which it is sedulously promoting in numerous markets. Some long-aged Japanese whisky is ridiculously costly, but most is comparatively cheap. The Japanese consume a great deal of their own whisky: those who can afford to, drink Scotch, but that is very heavily taxed in favour of the domestic version.

Since the First World War, when it was difficult to transport Scotch to the Antipodes, whisky has been made in Australia. The Second War gave it a greater encouragement. In Victoria in particular, conditions prevail which allow for the distilling of a perfectly acceptable and inex-

pensive alternative to blended Scotch. More recently, New Zealand has produced a good quality whisky.

In Europe, the Netherlands, with a very long tradition of distilling, makes a sound whisky. That of Spain can be adequate for mixed drinks, but the quality is less consistent.

A curiosity of recent years was the reintroduction of Welsh whisky – *Cymraeg Chwisgi*. Whisky was made in Wales in the 19th century: Queen Victoria, who liked Scotch, accepted a cask of it. The revived spirit, under the euphonious title Sound of the Waves (*Sŵn y Don*), was put on a limited distribution in 1978.

An illicit whiskey still in Donegal.

Cognac maturing in an ancient Hennessy chais.

BRANDY

Brandy is a word that without further qualification may be applied (under British law) only to distillations derived entirely from grapes and matured for three years. This is a broad definition since it covers production from sundry grape by-products. Consequently, the finest old Cognac and the poorest distillation from the umpteenth pressing of grapes qualify as brandies.

Brandy of varying sorts is made in every wine-producing country. The State of California distils more brandy than France, the country with which one instinctively associates the product.

For those who are interested in words,
brandy derives from the Dutch *brandewijn* (burned – i.e. distilled – wine), a tribute to the Netherlands as pioneer distillers. It was the English, who have an historic talent for linguistic distortion, who changed this to 'brandy-wine', which at one time was used for any distilled spirits. Shortened to brandy, the world adopted the term.

We will briefly explain brandy types.

Cognac

In prestige, the premier brandy is Cognac. To bear this title, a brandy must come from a very closely defined region and be made in a prescribed manner from specified grape varieties. We need not go into details of Cognac production beyond a few basic facts.

Cognac is twice distilled. It is aged in oak casks on a complicated system which involves building up average age by blending younger Cognac with older. The evaporation rate during prolonged maturing is high, one factor in making Cognac more expensive and better than lesser brandies.

The general description of standard Cognac is Three Star – though some companies employ a brand-name instead. This is the best brandy of all for Cocktails and mixes drinks: no-one would seriously think of employing a superior grade to Three Star.

The next grade up is usually called VSOP. This stands for Very Special Old Pale, though it is not paler than any other Cognac. The initials were introduced by the British trade many years ago when brandy tended to be darker than today. VSOP or other superior grades of Cognac are sometimes referred to as 'liqueur' brandy. By that it is understood that it is pleasant to drink undiluted (slightly warmed by a hand-held glass) after a meal: but the term is misleading in that 'liqueur' implies sweetness.

Beyond VSOP, moving into the rarer, costlier realms of Cognac, proprietors usually have their own designations for greater age, like X.O. or names peculiar to them. These superior Cognacs will also be described as *fine champagne* or *grande champagne*, giving rise to the highly misleading conversational phrase 'Champagne Cognac': there is no connection

whatsoever between Champagne and Cognac. *Champagne* is an ancient local Cognac description for a large space; i.e. vineyards.

The *grande champagne* is the most prestigious of the six regions into which the Cognac district is divided, and Cognac distilled from wine grown there is considered the best. The next is the *petite champagne*, rarely seen on labels. The other four divisions are of no general interest. Confusingly, the much esteemed *fine champagne* is not a location at all, but indicates a Cognac from both premier divisions, not less than half coming from the *grande champagne*. Vintage Cognac, of a single year and long matured in Britain, is rather a curiosity – not necessarily better than a first class, long aged blended Cognac. 'Napoleon' Cognac is a term without real meaning. It is employed on the labels of some very fine old Cognacs, but it is has no protection and anyone can use it on any brandy.

The British Connection

The Cognac area centres on the Charente River in South-West France, north of Bor-

deaux. This region was for three centuries a possession of the English Crown, from 1152 when Eleanor of Aquitaine brought it as part of her dowry on marrying Henry II. From that time on, regardless of ownership, wine – and later brandy – flowed from the region to Britain. Even war scarcely stopped it. Britain became – and in most years remains – the best market for Cognac. Britons, settling in the area, have become prominent names in the Cognac industry, such as Richard Hennessy, from Ireland, who set up as a distiller in 1765.

Armagnac

Second in commercial importance to Cognac is Armagnac. Some rate it superior – particularly the Gascons who make it. They tend to look on the Cognac distillers as successful newcomers, claiming themselves as the first French distillers of brandy. Being made in a comparatively remote part of the country, near the Pyrenees, and without the easy transport enjoyed by distillers along the Charente, Armagnac brandy remained for long a local spirit. Today it is showing a commercial cohesion that its highly individualistic producers failed to express in the past and Armagnac is much more widely available.

Armagnac is made, usually on a much smaller scale than Cognac, by a type of continuous still peculiar to the region. The resulting brandy is more robust in flavour than Cognac and benefits from longer maturing. The same grade indications – Three Star, etc. – are employed. Very distinctive Armagnac is to be relished after meals; few would consider it suitable for mixing.

Other Brandies

Apart from Cognac and Armagnac, France makes a great deal of spirit to which the term 'grape brandy' is often applied. In France, *fine* describes such brandy. Grape spirit may carry a label describing it as French brandy: we stress, it cannot be called Cognac (or Armagnac) unless it is fully entitled to those protected terms. Simple French grape brandy is usually sold under a brand-name. The same grade descriptions are often employed as for Cognac – VSOP, etc. and even 'Napoleon', plus such additions as 'de luxe', 'liqueur', 'special'. This can mislead the uninitiated.

That said, good grape brandy – French or from other places – is quite satisfactory for mixed drinks and represents some economy. German, Italian, Spanish and Greek brandies have their own characteristics, as do those of Cyprus. On their own, they probably taste more attractive in their countries of origin. To some palates a few may be a trifle too highly flavoured for the more delicate mixed drinks. South African brandy is an excellent mixing spirit; Australian is sound brandy but not much is exported.

Technically brandy is also the *marc* ('mar') of France; Italian *grappa*, German *trester*, Spanish *aguardiente de oruja*, or Portuguese *bagaceira*, and some South American *pisco* (Peruvian has a reputation). But these are usually roughish distillations from the final grape pressings – the sort of drink one tries out experimentally on holiday. However, *marc de Bourgogne* is exported and some folk say they enjoy it in place of a Cognac.

DARK RUM

In this category we include all rum but white, from golden to quite heavily coloured. These rums have a pungency which varies greatly. The most strongly flavoured is Navy rum: there are several brands. This is the most traditional of rums. The source of its description is obvious: it was the dark, powerful, once almost treacly spirit issued in the Royal Navy, and known as Nelson's Blood. The practice has been discontinued. Navy style rum was highly favoured by other sailors and was the preferred spirit in ports. Though less highly flavoured rum has to some extent replaced Navy rum, dark rum remains the favourite in seafaring communities and, indeed, in Britain it continues to outsell white rum, despite the increased popularity of the latter.

Since we dealt first with white rum, the basic method of producing rum was given then. In practical terms, nowadays all rum starts white (as do all spirits) and usually with little flavour – although it is possible to make rum with any degree of flavour by continuous distillation. Some very special rum is made by pot-stills, but most dark rum nowadays starts as lightly flavoured spirit into which is added a concentrated rum essence, condensed from molasses, according to the standards of the brand. The degree of colour is adjusted to conform to brand requirements.

Dark rums in normal trade are the same strength as whisky, but there are dark rums of up to double customary alcohols levels: these are not easily obtainable. Dark rum comes specially into its own in Punches, and people who do not care for dark rum on its own may find it very pleasant when its taste is blended with fruit juices and other ingredients. Dark rum also takes specially well to being heated.

CALVADOS

Calvados is colloquially referred to as brandy – apple brandy – but, as we have indicated, it is not brandy. Since it is matured and takes up some colour, it should here briefly be mentioned.

Calvados is not much drunk outside France. Its home is Normandy, the French cider country, and there it is drunk as aperitif, after meal digestif and as a break

COLOURED SPIRITS IN BRIEF

Whisky most usually indicates Scotch blended whisky. This is a mixture of pure malts (from malted barley) and the lighter grain (maize) whisky.

American whiskey's best-known style is Bourbon; it is based on maize. It is a constituent of several famous cocktails.

Canadian whisky is a light style; a good mixer.

Irish whiskey is the oldest. It has gained widespread modern popularity through Irish Coffee.

Brandy at best is distilled from special wine: Cognac is the premier type. 'Grape brandy' may be made from any grape by-products: superior styles are quite suitable for mixed drinks. ('Brandy' from sources other than grapes is not brandy: some are explained under both spirit sections.)

Dark rum is the traditional style. Degrees of pungency vary markedly. Excellent in numerous punches and mixed drinks.

Apples galore in the Normandy orchards.

during the rich local repasts. Well aged, it can be a splendid spirit, and it really deserves wider recognition. A similar American product (though not made in quite the same way) is known as Applejack.

Calvados is thought of as being distilled cider. It is not. A simple, rather rough cider *eau de vie* (spirit) is produced in Normandy: it is not proper Calvados, which is made by a more complicated process, with strict regulations. The basic fermentation from which Calvados is distilled is of mashed whole apples. The fluid from the fermentation of these is twice distilled, and the superior styles are rested in wood ten years or more.

The best Calvados is rather too good for mixed drinks, but if you have less expensive examples you could try using them in drink recipes calling for brandy. It will not give the same result but could be an interesting experiment.

'Fruit Brandy'

There is a huge range of what are known, non-technically, as 'fruit brandies'. Distilled from fruits other than grape they may not be called brandy in Britain. Though some examples have colour, for the most part these are white: they are dealt with briefly as an appendix to the white spirit section.

Cherry brandy is so called if the spirit into which the cherry-flavour is induced is grape spirit: the same applies to apricot and similar brandies. However, excellent 'cherry brandy' is made with other spirit.

2

Other Alcoholic Drinks

Other than spirits, there are sundry categories of drinks, of varying alcoholic strength, which play an important role in home drinking – the aspect of social drinking which is our prime concern. Whilst many are usually taken in their own right, a number of them also have relevance to cocktails and mixed drinks.

Nowadays made in many countries, Vermouth is historically associated with Italy and France. At one time it was usual to call Red (*rosso*) Vermouth 'Italian' and Dry Vermouth 'French'. The geographic description, as precisely denoting place of production, no longer pertains. Red and Dry are the terms we shall employ.

Bitter-sweet Red Vermouth is fairly close to the first commercial Vermouth which appeared in the 1780s. Before the introduction of bottled versions, Vermouth was sold as a concentrate, to be added to wine in the proportions preferred by the individual consumer.

In antiquity, the wormwood plant was known to have medicinal properties, particularly as a vermifuge – a remedy for intestinal parasites, for long centuries a scourge through widespread eating of infected food. The ancient Romans liked a wormwood-flavoured wine. Though the medicinal use of wormwood continued, it appears that only in Bavaria did at all a pleasing wine thus flavoured continue to be made. This *vermutwein* was discovered by an itinerant Italian in the 16th century. He introduced it into France, without any personal success, and brought his formula back to his home in Piedmont, in Northern Italy. There it evidently took hold, probably much modified by the addition of herbs in which the province was rich. Before the end of the 17th century *vermout* (the English had yet to add the 'h') was being praised for its salubrious properties. Though not yet named, before then 'wormwood wine' was known in London.

Red Vermouth

It was not until 1840 that Vermouth received its first legal recognition. By Royal proclamation, the vintners of Turin – then, as now, the focal point of Piedmontese Vermouth manufacture – were given protection against their imitators.

Red Vermouth became a favoured aperitif drink all over the world, and Italian firms

The harvesting of grapes for the production of Vermouth.

were soon to start making it in several countries. The word Vermouth is not itself protected internationally, as is, for instance, Scotch whisky. It is descriptive, but the industry is dominated by Italian names.

Red (*rosso*) Vermouth is based on a light white wine. Into this is infused a complicated formula of essences from a large number – up to fifty – of aromatic botanical elements which vary from one firm to another: the brand differences are easily distinguished. Sugar and colouring are added. After blending and resting, to ensure conformity of taste within the requirements of a given brand, the Vermouth is fortified with grape brandy to around 18% alcoholic strength, is refrigerated to remove wine deposits and further clarified by thorough filtering. This makes Vermouth extremely robust, capable of enduring wide temperature ranges without damage to its quality.

Red Vermouth has long featured in mixed drinks of longstanding popularity, as our recipes will demonstrate.

Dry Vermouth

Except that it is a herb-flavoured, fortified wine, Dry Vermouth has little in common with Red. It is unsweetened, light, and tends to be – and is often named – Extra Dry. It was evolved in the early 19th century: the first commercial firm to make it was founded in 1813 in Marseilles. The original Dry Vermouth was based on the sharp wines of the region. Wine for Dry Vermouth is matured in casks in the open, not in cellars. To this wine is added a blend of grape juice and grape brandy, along with certain herbs. After being well mixed

and rested, more wine is added and further grape brandy, the eventual strength of the Vermouth being 18–19% alcohol.

Dry Vermouth is less highly flavoured than it was before World War II. Its most traditional use was in the French national drink, Vermouth-Cassis (Dry Vermouth sweetened with blackcurrant cordial). It was, of course, what gave the *Dry* Martini its name: it is a constituent of other cocktails. Dry Vermouth is now much made in Italy, just as Red is produced in large amounts in France.

Other Vermouths

Bianco (White) Vermouth has enjoyed a considerable vogue in recent times, in keeping with the fashion for pale, rather bland, drinks. It is sweeter than Red Vermouth and has less pronounced a character. It is popular as a long drink with ice and a mixer like fizzy lemonade, but is rarely mentioned in cocktail recipes.

Casks of French Vermouth resting in the open air – an unusual feature of its production.

Very large blending casks in a traditional Vermouth winery.

Rosé Vermouth, a delicate pink, was introduced in modern times as a novelty. It had a remarkable success, possibly because it combines some of the characteristics of Red, with a little (but not all) of the sweetness of Bianco and the lightness of Dry. To many palates, it is delicious on its own, chilled. If one is to have just one Vermouth, one could use Rosé for most mixed drinks – except where dryness is essential.

Chambéry is a distinctive Vermouth from the Savoy department of France. Chilled Dry Chambéry is an esteemed aperitif drink. There are three other Cham-bérys: a Red, maybe rather insipid against traditional Red Vermouth; a bitter-sweet *Americano*-style, for drinking on ice with a slice of orange; and the unique dry *Chambéryzette*, flavoured with wild strawberries, not widely available but worth the search.

APERITIFS

Any drink taken before meals may be called an 'aperitif': the word remotely derives from the Latin for 'to open, or start'. Thus a cocktail, a pastis, or a Vermouth is an aperitif. However, conventionally, the term has more direct application to proprietary brands which either are labelled as aperitifs or have acquired that particular status.

Campari

This unique, internationally-celebrated Italian product demonstrates the difficulty of putting drinks into categories. It is often classed as a Vermouth: it is definitely not one, being much stronger, though it has vague taste similarity. Its own label description is 'bitters', but, though it is aromatically sharp, it is not what we usually call 'bitters'. It is most certainly an Aperitif, a fine appetiser. It has cocktail uses. On its own it is best drunk with ice, a round of orange and a splash of soda-water.

Carpano (Punt e Mes)

One might well include this under Vermouths, but its own description is *Aperitivo*. It is a splendid bitter-sweet, fortified wine drink that derives directly from the first commercial Vermouth. *Punt e Mes* was the Piedmontese dialect for 'point and a half', a *punt* being a local term for a measure of concentrated Vermouth essence, and one and a half of these became the accepted norm for adding to simple white wine. Signor Carpano based his formula on those proportions.

Amer Picon

A 'bitters' – its character owed to spirit, quinine, gentian and orange essence – but more usually served as an Aperitif, with ice and optional soda-water. Its tartness is sometimes cut by adding blackcurrant cordial.

Dubonnet-on-the-Rocks

Dubonnet

This is the best-known of French aperitifs. It was evolved a century and a half ago in Paris: now made in South-Western France. One of the early quinine-flavoured potions. We don't need quinine medicinally today, but the sharp taste, mellowed with sweetening, is attractive. Mixed red and white wines are the base, with a concentrate of red grape juice and spirit. Quinine bark is seeped in the treated wine whilst maturing. A Dry (*blond*) Dubonnet has been introduced in some world markets in supplement to the traditional red one.

St. Raphaël

Another famous quinine-flavoured wine aperitif, somewhat older than Dubonnet. The original, fairly heavily sugared red variety has been reinforced by pale Bianco version and by St. Raphaël Extra Dry which is light and has affinity to a Dry Vermouth.

Byrrh

The French drink that foreigners are advised, when ordering, to prefix with the word 'aperitif' to avoid getting a *bière* (beer). Sweetish, with quinine after-taste, and more popular in France than abroad.

Lillet

A herbal, fruit and (not much) quinine-flavoured wine, fortified with Armagnac brandy and well matured.

Ambassadeur

Comparatively new brand of aperitif from a noted liqueur firm; basic flavours are fruits and gentian, a bitter herb.

Suze

More strongly flavoured with gentian than any other aperitifs, this best-known of similar short drinks is sometimes listed as a Bitters. It is held to be a particularly good appetite promoter.

Kir

A proprietary bottled version of this famous and simple aperitif is available; see Miscellaneous Drinks (Chapter 9).

Fernet (Branca)

The Italians treat this mainly as an aperitif (and digestive), but we have decided to place it under Bitters.

Pineau

This is made by adding grape spirit to unfermented grape juice. The best known is *Pineau des Charentes*, from the Cognac region of France, but other wine areas produce their own.

Coconut is the taste from the Caribbean – a taste that conjures lazy days and magical nights.

Malibu can be drunk any time, straight on the rocks, or as a long drink. Lace it with cola, soda water, tonic or milk.

Tropical Coconut laced with light Jamaican Rum

Produced by
Twelve Islands Shipping Company Limited
1 York Gate, London NW1.

Malibu

This unique product is hard to classify. It has become immensely popular – taken at any time and in many ways. Its smart white bottle suggests its coconut content, which is blended with light rum.

LIQUEURS

Liqueurs are spirit-based, sweetened mixtures, those of great antiquity having medicinal origins in most instances. Their virtues are essentially digestive, though they are drunk after meals mainly because people find them delicious. Many are widely used in cocktails and mixed drinks.

Liqueurs are elaborately compounded, often from a large repertoire of ingredients. For that reason we have sparated them from 'white alcohol' and from single fla-

vour 'fruit brandy': these are considered in the white and coloured spirits section respectively. The term 'liqueur' is sometimes misleadingly applied – e.g. 'liqueur whisky', meaning a specially fine one: see Cognac. Because a drink is taken in what might be called 'a liqueur situation' – i.e after a meal – that does not make it a liqueur.

Liqueurs today embrace, for all practical purposes, several more mildly alcoholic cordials – some based on wine rather than spirit. It would be pedantic not to include them. There are quite modern ones that have achieved outstanding success. We also include *crèmes*, since they are closely related to true liqueurs.

The following alphabetical list does not pretend to be comprehensive: the world's liqueurs are innumerable. We believe these are the most interesting and important: they are nearly all stocked by, or available through, good off-licence stores.

Advocaat

Sweetened brandy, eggs and herbs. The word translates as 'lawyer'; the Dutch say the liqueur makes you as talkative as one.

Amaretto di Saronno

This popular Italian product, made from apricots and almonds, guards a romantic legend; that around 1525, the artist Luini used a beautiful widow as a model and she was so entranced with the portrait that she evolved the liqueur in his honour.

Anis, Anisette

A widespread range of highly aniseed-flavoured cordials.

The Abbey at Fécamp —
the home of Bénédictine.

Bailey's Original Irish Cream

Hugely successful, this is based on Irish whiskey, compounded with cream, chocolate and coffee. It has climbed into the top rank of popular liqueurs.

Bénédictine

Worldwide, possibly the number one liqueur. With political interruptions, it has been produced in the splendid monastery at Fécamp in Normandy since 1510. It is quite often taken mixed fifty-fifty with Cognac.

Chartreuse

The second most important French Liqueur originated by a religious order. It was evolved in the 17th century in the Carthusian monastery near Grenoble, a region rich in wild herbs. The expensive

Some of the twenty-seven herbs and spices needed to create Bénédictine.

An old time Cointreau poster.

Green Chartreuse is the very strong version: the Yellow is slightly weaker and more sweet.

Cointreau

By far the best known in the field of orange Curaçao (see below). It is synonymous with the best of this style of liqueur and, for clarity, we specify it in cocktails, as this brand-name is better recognised than the product.

Crèmes

The term describes a large number of very sugary cordials, often with low alcoholic strength. 'Cream' liqueurs, such as Bailey's, are in quite a different category: they are not *crèmes*. All sorts of flavourings are used for *crèmes* – nuts, rose petals, violets. The result is often sickly. There are three important *crèmes*:

Crème de Cacao

Heavily chocolate-flavoured; sometimes employed in sweet cocktails.

Crème de Cassis

This is the delicious, low strength, blackcurrant syrup particularly associated with the Burgundy country. It is a valuable flavouring agent in mixed drinks. See Syrups (blackcurrant).

Crème de Menthe

This is a true liqueur and a universally popular one. It is often poured on to

Overleaf: The magnificent Carthusian monastery near Grenoble whence come the Chartreuse liqueurs. ▶

55

Who said Drambuie was for after dinner only?

crushed ice and drunk through a straw. It frequently occurs in cocktails. Usually green, there is a slightly drier white variety.

Curaçao

Named after the Dutch Caribbean island which was the original source of a type of bitter orange used to make it, and therefore sometimes called 'orange Curaçao' ('cure-ah-so'). Now widely made. Usually white, though a coloured version, notably 'Blue Bols', is the only drink of any consequence of this hue. See 'Cointreau'.

Drambuie

The world-famous Scottish liqueur, based on fine Scotch whisky and flavoured with heather honey and herbs to a secret formula held by the Mackinnon family who, by legend, received it from Bonnie Prince Charlie after saving his life. The brandname is a contraction of the Gaelic for 'the drink that satisfies'.

Galliano

Yellow Italian herbal liqueur in the very tall bottle invented at the end of the last century and named after a military hero. It has enjoyed recently in the United States a remarkable success (largely as a modern cocktail ingredient) which has been to a considerable extent repeated in Britain.

Cherry Brandy

Grant's is the superior British brand. See also Peter Heering.

Glayva

Fairly modern Scotch liqueur with affinities to Drambuie.

Grand Marnier

Distinguished French liqueur about a century old, with a Curaçao flavour but based on Cognac, not simply *eau de vie*.

Irish Mist

Based on Irish whiskey, this liqueur claims ancestry from a honey wine (perhaps a mead) that features in Irish legends.

Irish Velvet

A blending of sugar, coffee and whiskey with which, by following simple instructions – including adding cream – one may make a sort of instant Irish Coffee.

Kahlua

The fine Mexican cane spirit liqueur heavily flavoured with coffee, giving character to several interesting mixes.

Kümmel

Of Baltic origin, but now much produced in the Netherlands and elsewhere. It is flavoured with caraway, aniseed and cumin, and is peculiarly highly prized as a digestive: one of those flavours much liked or heartily detested.

Malibu

Often favoured as a liqueur, its unusual flavour makes it very useful when a delicate touch of coconut is called for in a cocktail. (It is described earlier in this chapter.)

Mandarine

Mandarine Napoleon is the best-known of this type of tangerine-flavoured French liqueur. (There is also tangerine *crème* which is not the same thing at all.)

Maraschino

Originally made from marasca cherries peculiar to parts of what is now Yugoslavia. The type has been successfully grown in Italy. Good to enliven fruit salads and an excellent cocktail ingredient.

Parfait Amour

From its extreme stickiness might be called a *crème*, though it is a very old digestive liqueur from Western France. Today the best-known comes from the Netherlands. It is violet, almond-flavoured, scented and syrup-sweet.

Peter Heering's Cherry Liqueur

Usually still called by its earlier title, 'Cherry Heering'. This celebrated Danish product was introduced to London 150 years ago:

it is the internationally most popular Cherry brandy.

Royal Mint Chocolate

The title of this fairly new English liqueur, which has been well received, is wholly descriptive of its flavour.

Sambuca

Italian product with aniseed taste predominating. Usually served with coffee beans (*con mosche* 'with flies') which are set alight.

Southern Comfort

Powerful, delicately peach-flavoured American brand of liqueur. Sometimes erroneously confused with American whiskey: it is not one.

Strega

An extensive range of Italian liqueurs go under this name: their taste is basically lemon-orange.

Swedish Punsch

A well-spiced cordial, its origin obvious, drunk as a liqueur or hot toddy.

Tia Maria

Customarily served with cream floating on it, this coffee-flavoured Jamaican liqueur is immensely popular in Britain.

Van der Hum

The name translates roughly as 'what's-his-name'. This celebrated old South African product is basically tangerine-flavoured.

CIDER

Cider has showed a very steady growth in popularity in recent years. Some of this may be explained by its huge variety. The basic apple flavour is always there, but cider can be acid-sharp to fully sweet (and every variation between), strong, almost non-alcoholic, on draught, bottled, still, fizzy, or naturally sparkling ('champagne' cider). All tastes are catered for.

As a mixer, cider has considerable merit, particularly in summer punches and coolers. A medium-sweet, still cider is the most useful general purpose one. A sparkling cider (Pomagne Dry is the best) is sometimes a perfectly adequate substitute for sparkling wine.

BEER

What Beer is bought for the home is obviously very much a matter of individual taste. Dark ale and stout are the only beers much called for in mixed drinks.

WINE

It is not the function of this book to deal with wine except in relation to cocktails and mixed drinks. No-one is seriously going to use fine wines for such purposes: one simply requires sound and suitable ones. Today that usually means good blended brand-name wines, offering a broad selection of types, as in the Carafino range.

Where white wine is mentioned in a recipe, unless a dry wine is very specifically

OTHER DRINKS IN BRIEF

Vermouth is the most important of aperitifs. The leading styles are bitter-sweet red, and dry. Bianco (white) Vermouth is sweeter.

Aperitif refers to any drinks taken as appetisers, but more particularly to certain proprietary brands other than Vermouths, which are Aperitif drinks but dealt with separately: so are spirits like pastis/Pernod.
    The best-known brand-name aperitifs in Britain are Campari and Dubonnet.

Liqueurs are sweetened, flavoured alcohols, and very numerous. Favourites in the UK are (alphabetically):
Advocaat; Bailey's Irish Cream; Benedictine; Chartreuse; cherry brandy; Crème de Menthe; Cointreau; Drambuie; Malibu; Southern Comfort; Tia Maria.

Wine is mentioned in this book solely in relation to mixed drinks; only basic medium-dry white, red and sparkling wines are of any considerable importance in this context.

Cider may replace wine in some mixed drinks.

mentioned, a medium-dry will cover all requirements. For red wine drinks, any reasonably robust one suffices: if too thin, the resultant drink will lose character.

Sparking wines play a considerable role in stimulating cold Punches, so admirable for out-door entertainment. Undeniably, non-vintage Champagne will give the best results. But let us be realistic: some other naturally sparkling wines will do very well. In our recipes we shall only specify Champagne when to use something else would ruin the drink. Where we only mention sparkling wine, without alternative, we are indicating that to use Champagne would be positively wasteful.

Naturally sparkling wines (as opposed to slightly cheaper, artifically carbonated ones) are recommended as the artificially effervescent ones quickly go flat. French sparkling wines tend to be drier than the

German *sekt* or Italian *spumante*, of which the Asti is the best. However, both those countries, as well as France, make *brut* (very dry) sparkling wines. *Moscato* (Muscat) *spumante* is decidedly sweet and usually carbonated. The quality and taste range of sparkling wines is large. If you have no established preference, seek advice when purchasing and mention your intended purpose.

Port features in quite a few good mixed drinks. We suggest something like a Croft's Ruby. True Port is recommended, rather than 'port style' from other countries.

With drinks calling for sherry, in most instances an Amontillado is satisfactory, being neither too dry nor too sweet. A Cyprus sherry, medium dry, will serve almost as well.

Sundry Ingredients

3

Apart from the Spirits or Wines, there are certain items which the home entertainers will require in preparation of Cocktails and mixed drinks. We place a * against the most generally useful Bitters, Syrups and Juices.

BITTERS

Angostura*

Chief and most versatile of bitters are Angostura. These also have uses in cooking and so many households keep them. For many years they carried heavy tax, because of their high alcohol content: Angostura are now classified as food flavouring and escape the long arm of HM Customs and Excise. This relief caused a dramatic price reduction.

Angostura bitters were invented by Dr. J. G. B. Siegert, whose family still controls them. The doctor prepared his aromatic compound after studying the herbal medicaments of Indians. He established a company in the Venezuelan town of Angostura (since re-named) in 1823. Shortly afterwards, production moved to Trinidad.

Orange Bitters

Bitter-orange peel essence in weak alcohol, mildly sweetened.

Campari*

See Aperitifs.

Fernet (Branca)

This powerfully sharp form of bitters is in Britain mainly taken as a 'morning-after' restorative and features in Pick-Me-Up Cocktails. Branca is the best-known of Italian brands of *fernet*, a fluid originally brewed from many herbs by religious recluses in the Alps.

Underberg

The curative, strong bitters, enormously popular in Germany, which have gained a strong allegiance in Britain amongst those who find them a prime settler of queasy stomachs.

SYRUPS

Sugar Syrup*

You can buy *sirop* (Gomme) made from unrefined cane sugar, or very simply make something virtually the same.

Boil 250 g (½-pound) granulated white sugar in 50 cls (½-pint) water. Bottle and store in refrigerator (not freezer) where it will last almost indefinitely. Where a recipe demands 'sugar', this syrup may be employed in exactly the same stated quantities.

Blackcurrant syrup*

This is a household article, and is much used in mixed drinks. Best to use true syrup – Ribena is the prime example – and not a 'blackcurrant drink'. This is an acceptable non-alcoholic substitute for Crème de Cassis (see Liqueurs).

Peppermint Cordial

Grenadine*

This is a particularly delightful syrup, much used in mixed drinks, and those unfamiliar with it are recommended to try it. It is delicately flavoured with pomegranates.

Rose Hip*

Another household article, this delicious syrup is, some aver, much too good for the children for whom it is designed! Be that as it may, although the flavour is different, it may be used as an unorthodox but interesting alternative to Grenadine as a sweetener-flavouring agent.

JUICES

Lime Juice Cordial*

For cocktails, you will get best results by using real lime juice cordial (Rose's) rather than 'lime flavour' drinks, though the latter may be employed for economy in cold punches where a large quantity is needed.

Lime Juice

Lime juice must not be confused with lime juice cordial, which is sweetened. Lime juice is extremely sharp. Fresh limes being rather scarce in Britain, in all appropriate recipes we give lemon juice as a highly satisfactory alternative. Rarely is pure lime juice imperative.

Lemon Juice*

Plays a big part in mixed drinks. Pure bottled lemon juice is perfectly in order, but make quite sure it is the *unsweetened* variety, sometimes marked 'sharp'. If you press your own juice, it will keep under refrigeration.

Orange Juice*

As important as lemon juice. Quality pure, *unsweetened* orange juice (frozen or in carton, can or bottle) is suitable for mixed drinks. Concentrates and 'long life' styles are not ideal for Cocktails. Nothing can beat freshly pressed orange juice: as with lemon, this may be stored under deep refrigeration.

Tomato Juice*

In small bottles if you are unlikely to use much; otherwise in jars, cans or cartons.

Pineapple Juice

Increasingly popular: surplus liquid from canned pineapple is worth preserving for use in drinks.

Grapefruit Juice (unsweetened)

Passion Fruit

Bottles and can are not readily available, but if you find this delicious juice, try it. It goes very well with Gin.

Apple Juice and Grape Juice

These are attractive, but have only ancillary minor applications.

'Squashes' are not satisfactory in cocktails: top quality fruit drinks may be used in some punches, though we rarely list them.

MISCELLANEOUS

In several instances, items that are almost essential for mixing drinks are already in many homes, e.g.:

Worcester Sauce, Cayenne Pepper, Salt, Sugar (lump and caster; white and brown), *Fizzy lemonade, Tonic Water, Soda-Water, Ginger Ale, Cola, Bitter Lemon, Lemons* and *Oranges.*

Where the rind of lemons or oranges is to be used in drinks, it is desirable to wash them to remove any preservatives: these are harmless but could slightly taint a delicate mix.

Optional, yet valuable, ingredients to have to hand are:

Cocktail Cherries. Marashino cherries are best. Preserve the liquid as a sweet flavouring.
Pearl Onions. Tiny pickled onions, sometimes called cocktail onions.

Green Olives. Not too large. Don't use the stuffed type in mixes, though they are pleasant to nibble with drinks.

Powdered Nutmeg
Cinnamon Sticks
Tabasco Sauce

ICE & WATER

Ice is so important to drink mixing that it deserves special mention.

You cannot make really good drinks with poor ice. Poor ice? Well, if your local water is so highly treated that you think it rather unpalatable, then the ice you make from it will retain most of those characteristics. You may find the minor extravagance of buying still spa water is justified. Such waters, and natural or artificial sparkling ones, have enjoyed a boom in Britain, where they were once little used in comparison to their regular household employment on the Continent. A Whisky-and-Polly (Apollinaris, the German natural sparkling water) was fashionable, but no longer. The Americans, apt to indulge in crazes, have gone overboard for Perrier (France's answer to 'Polly'), treating it as a smart aperitif. It is known that the Queen drinks Malvern water, taking it with her on journeys abroad. There is now a consider-able range of British and imported spa waters: the name derives from the Belgium town of Spa, first to commercialise its pure spring product. For ice, do not use *pétillant* (faintly effervescent) waters, nor those with pronounced, if healthful, mineral tang.

Ice from the domestic refrigerator is 'softer', less lasting, than commercial ice. If you have a freezer, you can make splendid ice by putting water into a clean, clear plastic bag or container, allowing room for expansion. To break up the block, wrap in a cloth and bash with a mallet on a hard surface. To make crushed ice – pleasant for many drinks – simply continue the process until there remain no sizeable lumps.

When we refer in a recipe to a cube of ice, we mean the sort of little block you get from an ice-tray or piece of equivalent volume.

If using fairly large bits of ice in a mixing glass or shaker, you can rinse them well and use again for another style of drink without carrying over unwanted flavour from the previous mix.

To prevent ice pieces congealing together in a bowl, squirt a little soda-water over them.

For non-alcoholic mixes, and to doll up soft drinks for children, you can make multi-hued ice cubes by putting a few drops of flavourless food colouring in the water.

4

What is a Cocktail?

In case you are a person who does not read introductions to books, deeming that 'starter' unimportant and preferring to go straight on to the main course, it seems worth briefly recapitulating something previously mentioned. That is that we are experiencing a new 'Cocktail Age', but one very different to the earlier and frankly rather silly one. The new fashion for cocktails knows no social boundaries. It illustrates a more catholic approach to drinking, which probably owes much to the vogue for foreign travel affecting all levels of society. Further, home entertainment has been revolutionised: hospitality has become more imaginative. On a broad scale, people are showing an initiative in this activity, once confined to a minute spectrum of the populace. We have also indicated that making cocktails is neither difficult nor necessarily expensive. It can provide a lot of fun.

Interestingly, what a cocktail truly is has never been officially defined. One might expect that by now there would have been a test case to establish a legal description, since a 'cocktail' is, in a public place, deemed exempt from the regulations setting the minimum quantities of whisky, gin, vodka, and rum (not, curiously, brandy) that may be served in a bar. It is generally accepted that a mix containing at least three ingredients is classed as a Cocktail, but this is not much help when no-one has decided that constitutes an ingredient: is a single drop of bitters an ingredient? For that matter, is ice? A sliver of lemon rind? But these are no more than discussion points.

Long before the word 'cocktail' gained general currency, our ancestors were drinking mixes to which precise name categories were allocated – Daisies, Fixes, Cups, Slings, Twists, Swizzles, Sours, Crusta, Cobblers: those are a few of them. An American book on mixing drinks published in 1882, in the author's library, does not have the word 'cocktail' in its title and it is rarely used in the text or recipes. Some of the old terms are incorporated in the names of drinks still made today, but cocktail has become the all-embracing term. We shall use it to cover nearly all the drinks in our recipes section, except for obvious exception like punches. A cocktail is essentially an individual, not a bulk, drink.

Nothing New

In a drinking connection, the word cocktail appears first in an American journal of 1806: 'a stimulating liquor composed of spirits of any sort, sugar, water and bitters'. However, mixed drinks were widespread long before then. Centuries ago, wine was being mixed with all sorts of things – medicinally, or often simply to make vile wine drinkable. It would be fanciful to call those

Even the Parisiennes followed the Americans craze for cocktails.

cocktails, but the Negus, popular in Queen Anne's reign, might well qualify for inclusion.

Charles Dickens discovered the cocktail on an American visit and the first use of the word by an English author is probably that in his *Martin Chuzzlewit* (1843). Well over a century ago, Americans were drinking a wide variey of cocktails, but, though mixed drinks were not unknown in Britain, they were not often described as cocktails. In fact, the word was for long derogatory. Writing of the year 1901, when John Galsworthy (*The Forsyte Saga*) wished to emphasise a character's caddishness, he had him taking a cocktail at an inappropriate moment. After the first World War, the cocktail habit did spread to Britain from the U.S.A. – indeed to smart cosmopolitan society worldwide – but there remained something faintly shocking about it. It was considered very daring of the fashionable playwright Frederick Lonsdale to have the first cocktail served on the English stage in 1925. The rising Noël Coward was shortly to go one better in his highly alcoholic comedy *Fallen Angels* in which four distinct cocktails strongly featured. The cocktail scene was a glossy one, the restricted world of gossip-writers and the glamourous arena of film stars and ephemeral celebrity: old High Society were displeased with such goings-on. The mainstream of the population read about the cocktail-drinking Bright Young Things – remember the word Flapper? – but rarely tried to ape their foolish behaviour. Yet cocktails became indelibly associated with sophistication (which originally meant corrupt and adulterated) and the fashionable.

During the 1920s and early 'thirties, when cocktails reigned in this limited, highly publicised sphere, the United States were indulging in that extraordinary 'great experiment' called Prohibition. This gave immense stimulus to the already well-established U.S. custom of cocktail-drinking. There was an actual need to invent mixes which could make tolerable the horrors of hooch – illicit distillations frequently of noxious character. Even those with the money to buy good bootlegged liquor competed, quite unnecessarily, in concocting weird cocktails. Mercifully, very few of these have survived. Many excellent cocktails have come to us from pre-Prohibition days: only a few that were evolved during it are being drunk nowadays. However, American influence is enormously strong in the world's drinking patterns, and a very high proportion of cocktails popular today started across the Atlantic. How simple yet full of flavour they are compared to the witches brews of the 'twenties.

What's In A Name?

It is odd that a word in such international use has no known origin. 'Cocktail' is, when one analyses it, in no way obvious; neither cocks nor tails have any relation with it. It might be amusing – and cocktails are an amusing way of drinking – to examine a few theories. Let us start with the author's preferred origination, on the grounds of probability, though this by no means establishes a cut-and-dried case.

In the 18th century in England, it was usual to dock the tails of sound horses that were not thoroughbreds. Such animals were described as 'cocktailed' or as being a 'cocktail'. Horsey circles were notably hard-drinking. They imbibed plenty of punches and other mixes. Thus a drink that was not straight – one might say, not thoroughbred – was given the description applied to a horse of mixed ancestry. It became a 'cocktail drink'. It would be entirely logical for the term to have migrated to the United States.

Diverse other theories persist as to cocktail's verbal beginnings. They may strike the reader as more legendary than possi-

WANT A REAL HANGOVER?

There are many extraordinary cocktails which certainly have no place amongst the practical recipes in this book. Take 'Brain Buster', appreciated by old-time prospectors in the Australian gold fields: it consisted of equal measures of gin, rum, and a blend of opium and red pepper.

'Jelly Beans' was a cocktail unknown to the world outside Glasgow until, in the late 1970s, the consumption of it was given by the accused as an explanation for a minor theft he committed, i.e. the stealing of a glass from a bar. Asked by the court for the constituents of Jelly Beans, the defendant listed the ingredients: whisky, Pernod, gin, vodka, cherry brandy, lemonade and Babycham.

ble. Some pretty myths must be dismissed through unacceptable dating.

A notion at least as satisfactory as the one mentioned above is that cocktail derives from Cock-Ale, a strong concoction given to fighting cocks, two hundred years ago and more, to encourage them to battle. It was sometimes the custom to drink a toast to the winning bird with as many ingredients in the potion as it had tail feathers remaining: from Cock-Ale to cocktail?

Perhaps the most absurd cocktail story concerns the beautiful daughter of a Mexican chieftain. She was called Xcotl (spellings vary), and when some officers in the early U.S. Navy paid a courtesy visit on her father, she served them with delightful drinks. The visitors said they would commemorate their pleasant trip by titling equally interesting mixes after her. The nearest they could get to her tongue-twisting name – you've guessed – 'cocktail'.

Or is cocktail a corruption of *coquetel*, an ancient mixed drink of the Bordeaux region brought to America by French volunteer officers serving under General Washington during the War of Independence?

From the same hostilities comes the folk tale of Betsy Flanagan. She kept an inn much used by French volunteers fighting with the American, against the British. She had as neighbour a suspected Loyalist, who kept superior chickens to Betsy's. One day Betsy took some fowls, whose owner she considered a traitor, and fed them to French volunteers billeted on her, decorating the dish with tail feathers. Drinking their

◄ **Smart New Yorkers hold a wake to mourn the introduction of prohibition.**

hostess's health, the soldiers shouted, in an early instance of Franglais, 'Vive le cocktail', adding to the vocabulary of the new republic.

The Gallic influence continues later, in New Orleans, where it is recorded that a Frenchman, a chemist, experimented with mixed drinks which he eccentrically served in those double egg-cups known as *coquetiers*, which his American friends roughly translated as . . . need we say.

That is by no means the end of Cocktail fables, but enough to provide some conversational stimulus to your own mixing.

Inevitably, over the years, a considerable mystique has grown up around cocktails. Sundry rules have been promulgated. Pay no attention. There is no mystery to cocktails beyond what you personally care to invest in them. The author was once positively instructed by an ardent American addict to the Dry Martini that it must be stirred exactly two hundred times, one hundred in each direction. A trial run of this bit of bar lore produced a very watery cocktail.

To lay down laws about cocktails is ridiculous. To give, and take, advice on them is sensible: that we shall do. The very word cocktail, its origins locked in the past, carries a certain aura of magic – enticing, slightly exciting. The names of cocktails are often alluring, or amusing, or intriguing. They may also be confusing: under some titles, different authorities can give very varied recipes. Not to worry. The business of mixing drinks is really entirely straightforward. Children could easily make cocktails: we just have to hope they will leave that fun to the adults.

Cocktail Equipment

5

One could certainly make nearly any cocktail or other mix in this book using no other equipment than that to be found in a normal domestic kitchen. You *could* – but would you really *want* to?

So we cannot say that any of the following instruments are truly essential. However, most are distinctly useful, and practical.

Cocktail Shakers

There are two basic types:

1. By far the most popular cocktail shakers for home use are the standard three-piece ones. The most practical are made in stainless steel: silver-plated ones are attractive but you do have to polish them. There are also three-piece, sometimes two-piece, shakers combining metal and glass: we do not recommend them.

A standard three-piece shaker consists of main body, and a top section which contains strainer and sealing-cap. Into the body are put the ingredients and ice. The top section is then carefully slotted, ensuring a close fit and the cap in position. After shaking (see next chapter), the shaker's cap is removed and the drink strained into glasses.

2. The professional shaker – the Boston – has only two parts, usually a glass main body and a top metal section of almost the same capacity. But wholly metal Boston shakers are quite usual. The ingredients are placed in one of the cones, the other section slotted into it and the cocktail is ready for shaking. The two sections are then parted – and that can be quite a trick – and the drink is filtered through a separate strainer.

The Strainer

By far the most popular model, used to ensure the ice employed to chill the drink does not go into the glass, is the Hawthorn. This is a perforated metal disc surrounded by a flexible coil, with a short handle. This coil ensures a close fit into the body of Boston shaker or mixing glass.

Mixing Glasses

These are also called bar glasses. They are available in a confusing variety of shapes and sizes, in plain glass, cut glass, clear or coloured or decorated, with or without handles (usually without). All a mixing glass is, effectively, is a medium-sized jug. Personal taste must guide selection, but we make the following recommendations:

A sensible mixing glass should be between 1 pint (575 ml) and 1½ pints (850 ml) capacity, in plain or very lightly decorated glass.

It will stand between 6 and 9 inches high. The top will be about 3¾ inches in diameter: any purpose-made mixing glass will be around this size to accommodate the Hawthorn strainer.

Not all mixing glasses have a lip, but it does make for easier pouring.

A mixing glass with a plated rim holding a built-in strainer can look pleasing, but they are not entirely practical because of the difficulty of keeping them clean where metal and glass join.

Scrupulous cleanliness is a cardinal rule with bar equipment.

Bar Spoons

Though you own plenty of spoons nine to eleven inches long, they will not properly replace a bar spoon for the bowls will be clumsily large. A bar spoon has a tiny bowl in relation to its length. Again, you can obtain this bit of equipment in many forms

and metals; and, again, we recommend a plain model in stainless steel. A bar spoon needs to be robust, for its prime purpose is to be used vigorously in stirring ice with ingredients in a mixing glass. It may also be useful in getting olives out of jars, and similar activities.

Glass stirring rods have the virtue of extreme simplicity and ease of cleaning. However, they may not stand up to brisk mixing.

The base of a cocktail shaker can function as a mixing glass. So if you do not want both, opt for a shaker.

All Cocktails can be shaken; some cannot really satisfactorily be made by stirring.

However, the four basic pieces of equipment above need not be costly: you will find them very handy.

Measures

There are various ways in which you can measure spirits and other ingredients. (The average domestic egg-cup holds just on 1 fl. oz, but we will suggest other instruments.)

1. Measure-pourers, the globular attachments which fit on top of bottles. They are of modest reliability.
2. 'Non-drip' optics (which frequently do drip) as used in public houses. They are fairly expensive. You need brackets. As to reliability: ask your local pub landlord.
3. Old-fashioned 'pearl' optics, worked by a lever. Some of these are collector's pieces. They also need brackets.

All else apart, objections to 1–3 above lie in complication of maintenance. We strongly suggest that you use

4. Simple bar measures. There is nothing to go wrong. They are inexpensive and easy to clean. All you need is a reasonably steady hand.

A good type is a dual measure. Used one side it gives a 'single' and on the other a 'double'. A basic 1 fl. oz/25 ml measure is all you absolutely require.

You can buy ⅙ of a gill measures (the quantity of a 'single' in England), which is rather a mean amount. Or you can have the generous ¼-gill one, the so-called

Ice tongs, mould, bucket and ice crusher.

'club measure'. We find 1 fl. oz/25 ml the most convenient unit. Bar measures are usually in steel or silver–plate, though sometimes hygienic glass is used.

Glasses

The range of cocktail glasses is bemusing. The current vogue is for glasses favoured in the 1920s–30s, particularly the V-shaped ones. Often these are very wide at the top, making them none too practical.

Glassware is so much a question of per-sonal taste that we can do no more than say that all you need (and may already have) are:

Stemmed 'cocktail glasses'
Stemmed wine-glasses (serving as 'large cocktail glasses')
'Goblets', short-stemmed large wine-glasses
'Tumblers', like small traditional whisky tumblers.
'Tall glasses', for long drinks.

We go into matters of capacity in the intro-duction to recipes. The design of glasses is

These and all other equipment illustrated in this chapter are part of the William Levene Cocktail Makers Range.

for individual discretion: fairly plain, clear ones, showing the colour of the mix, have an aesthetic plus for many experts.

Other Items

Though most of the following useful items, or adequate substitutes, probably exist in the household, it may be found convenient to have a set of them kept separately from kitchenware – alongside the shaker and/or mixing glass.

1. A 'waiter's friend' – a combination of corkscrew, bottle-opener and knife.

2. A really sharp stainless steel knife with around 3–4 inch blade. (The knife in the 'waiter's friend' (1) will usually only be good for cutting foil on bottles.) An efficient knife is required for cutting fruit and paring peel from lemons.

3. A small wooden cutting-board.

4. Some form of fruit press.

5. Cocktail-cherry sticks and drinking straws.

6. An ice-bucket (preferably insulated) with tongs.

7. A drip tray for measures.

b) An electric blender: it must be a robust one or ice can damage it.

c) A patent stopper for re-closing sparkling wine bottles if only part of contents have been used.

d) Silver-plated professional pourers. These give a quick, clean pour. Plastic ones are not normally so practical. Pourers, after use, should not be left in bottles but washed and corks replaced. This stops evaporation and entry of insects, many of which love spirits as much as they do juices and cordials.

e) An electric ice-crusher: a low priority as equipment goes.

If you already have a home bar or cocktail cabinet, we do not need to tell you how many gadgets there are in the way of drink accessories. If you are newly embarking upon the craft of 'mixology' initially resist the temptation to buy more than basic equipment. You can always elaborate later if you wish. Practicality should take precedence over decoration, but the false economy of shoddy equipment is to be avoided: buy less but buy better. The author has seen a silver ice-bucket (only fairly practical) at £600: he uses a very sensible brand-advertising one that cost him nothing!

Optional Luxuries

a) Small glass bitters bottles, with plated drip-control closure. These can also be used for, say, Pernod: they make it easier to give a 'dash' of an ingredient.

Shaking and Stirring

It is customary to employ a shaker for cocktails containing fruit juices, heavy liqueurs, and particularly those with cream, for thorough mixing is required which can less easily be procured by stirring in a bar glass.

The extra palaver of using a shaker is not necessary for drinks that have no special ingredients other than those which blend easily.

We do not believe in too many 'rules'. However, there are certain guidelines worth considering:

It is desirable to wrap a clean white cloth round shakers. Not only are they frigid to the touch: they often tend to 'weep' at the seams.

Do not more than three-quarters fill a shaker, nor try to make too many servings at one shaking.

A mixing glass may be filled nearer to the top than a shaker. Leave room to stir without spillage: if brimful, there will not be space for the strainer and the drink will be difficult to pour.

Do not fill glasses to the brim, either. This is a bar habit to give an impression of generosity. It simply makes for spilling. Better to use a slightly larger glass: your guests' hands may not be as steady as yours.

If you have some of a mix left in shaker or mixing glass, do not leave the ice in it for, as it melts, it will dilute the cocktail excessively. Pour off the drink into a jug: you can add it to further mixing of the same recipe. Before re-filling utensils, pour away the water from any residual ice. If making up a different recipe, wash shaker and take fresh ice (you can wash and re-use previously used ice). We have dealt with ice in Chapter 3.

It has become the fashion to garnish modern cocktails with redundant fruit and all sorts of inedible embellishments – fancy stirring sticks, gimmick straws, garish miniature parasols and so on. In some bars it is quite difficult to uncover the drink itself! The extent to which you wish to indulge in this practice is up to individual taste.

It would be silly to give suggestions that cocktails should be mixed with the ice for any given time. Obviously the longer, and more quickly, you shake or stir, the colder

– and weaker – the drink will be. This is a matter for commonsense, remembering that a watery cocktail is not a very good one.

With drinks served on-the-rocks, it is again a question of personal taste how much ice is used. The usual way is to mix the recipes normally, and then pour into goblet or tumbler about one-third filled with pieces or cubes of ice. But some people like more, others less. Certain drinks served on-the-rocks are made in the glass from which they will be drunk. In a few cases, the entire contents of shaker, including the ice, are poured into the serving glass.

On-the-rocks is not quite the same as serving a drink on crushed ice (see Chapter 3). The usual term for a drink

served with crushed (sometimes called 'Snow') ice is *frappé*, of which *crème de menthe frappé* is the best-known example. That is not, of course, a cocktail: the liqueur is simply poured into a small stemmed glass that is almost filled with finely crushed ice, and drunk through a straw.

Frosting the rim of cocktail glasses has lately become very popular. Drinks thus served used to be called Crustas, a term now almost archaic. If you wish, you may serve virtually any *sweet* cocktail in this manner. Put a thin layer of caster sugar on a plate; moisten the rim of the glass with iced water (or lemon juice) and touch it to the sugar. For Tequila cocktails, use lemon juice, and, with some exceptions, salt in place of sugar.

If – a fairly big if – you are so well equipped that you have a refrigerator in your 'home bar' or beside your cocktail cabinet, and if you have the space in it, glasses kept in it will frost all over. This gives lustre to a clear, pale cocktail (notably the Dry Martini). You remove the glass from refrigerator immediately before straining the drink into it.

Simple Conversions

In Britain we are at a stage where there are many young adults who have been brought up to recognise (with some exceptions) metric standards, while there is a larger section of mature persons who continue to operate mentally mainly in Imperial measures. The former group still know miles better than kilometres and the latter are coming to terms with grammes and kilos, but the generation gap is sharply defined when it comes to fluid measurement. So we give recipes (next chapter) in plain numerals, which as has been explained and you will be reminded about, refer to a basic measure of 1 fluid ounce or 25 millilitres.

To give entirely accurate conversions between Imperial and metric systems can involve going to four decimal places! We have rounded them out to sensible approximations. In the context of this book extensive tables serve no purpose.

Capacity measures

Imperial	Metric
1 gallon (160 fl. ozs)	= 4.5 litres
1 pint (4 gills)	= 5.75 cl (575 ml)
1 gill (¼-pint)	= 150 ml
1 fl. oz	= 25 ml

Metric	Imperial
1 litre	= 1¾ pints
½ litre (500 ml)	= 14 fl. ozs
150 ml	= 5 fl. ozs (¼ pint)
25 ml	= 1 fl. oz

Spoons (level)	Metric
¼ teaspoon (tsp)	= 1 ml
½ tsp	= 2.5 ml
1 tsp	= 5 ml
1 tablespoon (tblsp)	= 15 ml

Weight

Grammes	Ounces
1 kilogram	34 ounces (2.2 pounds)
500 g (½ kg)	18 ozs
100 g	4 ozs (¼ pound)
25 g	1 oz
12 g	½ oz

7 Recipes

We have previously mentioned that *cocktail titles* may be found in relation to mixes that have little connection. For instance, the author has uncovered seven different versions of the Bronx, a simple and celebrated gin cocktail for most people familiar with it – yet one of these 'Bronxes' prescribed whiskey. Naturally, we give the orthodox recipe. In instances where there are widely accepted variations in standard recipes, we indicate options. We have also introduced new mixes which will not be found in any other books. In effect, to speak of a 'new' cocktail, one is really talking of an adaptation. There are about 10,000 published recipes, though – mercifully – they have never been collected in one volume. In any event, it would be out of date by the time it was finished: new, or allegedly new, cocktails are evolved every day. Few indeed will be remembered the day after their inception, or deserve to be.

With a few light-hearted exceptions, our selection of Cocktails has been founded on practicality and commonsense.

The instructions '*Shake*' and '*Stir*' are used in recommendation only: they are not mandatory. In nearly all instances, either procedure will suffice. If it be particularly desirable to employ one method, as in 'Shake briskly', this is indicated, and, where other means of making a drink are necessary, these are clearly set out.

'*With ice*' means the use of ice cubes or small pieces. When '*crushed ice*' (see Chapter 3) is mentioned, it is preferably and usual to employ it. '*On-the-rocks*' implies – it is a useful Americanism – that the serving glass contains pieces of ice.

'*Frosting*' of the rims of glasses is explained in the previous chapter (6).

We mentioned *glasses* generally in Chapter 5. Broadly –

'Cocktail glass' refers to a small stemmed glass of approximately 3–4 fl. ozs (75–100 ml).

'Large cocktail glass' is around 4–6 fl. ozs, say 125–175 ml.

'Goblet' means a short-stemmed glass of some 7 fl. ozs (200 ml).

'Tumbler' indicates a non-stemmed glass about the same size as a goblet.

'Tall glass' is any suitable one for a long drink, 10 (½ pint) – 14 fl. ozs (up to 450 ml).

Recipes (with a few obvious exceptions) are given in terms of single servings. Most of them can, by multiplying ingredients proportionately, be made up to provide more individual drinks. How many, is a

matter of commonsense. Because a drink is a Long one, that does not preclude it being prepared for several people: its size may be governed by additions in the serving glass.

Unique to this book

1. For easy recognition, a number of recipes are marked with a *. These, including some long popular, are fairly simple.

2. 'C' signifies a Classic – a cocktail which, for a century or only a decade, has achieved widespread approval. (Allocation of Classic status is unofficial.)

3. To show at a glance the size-type of a drink, where appropriate they are coded:
   S. = Short (the sort normally served in an average cocktail-glass).
   L. = Long (in quantity, a substantial drink).
   ML. = Medium-long (as for a wineglass, large cocktail-glass or tumbler).

4. Further to make recipes helpful, a broad explanation is appended in many instances. This is intended mainly to show degrees of sweetness. A majority of the mixes most popular today are on the sweet side.

Such annotations are not applied to Hot Drinks, Party Drinks, Restorative Cocktails and Non-Alcoholic Drinks: they are used in Chapter 8.

Recipes are divided into categories. In particular this will be convenient for people with strong preferences for – or dislike of – certain spirits or other products as a base for their mixed drinks. Within the categories, listings are alphabetical:

White Spirits –
Gin cocktails
Vodka cocktails
White rum cocktails
Tequila cocktails

Coloured Spirits
Scotch whisky cocktails
Other whisk(e)y cocktails
Brandy cocktails
Dark rum cocktails

Cream cocktails
Sundry spirit cocktails
Party drinks & punches
Hot mixes
Non-spirit cocktails
Non-alcoholic drinks
Restorative cocktails

Chapter 8 deals with a few slightly more ambitious recipes, a few rather expensive ones or requiring unusual ingredients.

Certain important drinks which do not naturally fall into the categories above are covered in Chapter 9.

MEASURES

The unit of measure used throughout is based on a 'single' of 1 fl. oz/25 ml. That is our *standard measure* in recipes, except where otherwise stated.

To improve clarity, fl. oz and ml will not constantly be repeated. Quantities are expressed in number of *standard measures* for example:
1 Scotch whisky
2 Dry Vermouth
        meaning
One standard measure (1 fl. oz/25 ml) of Whisky
two standard measures (2 fl. ozs/50 ml) of Vermouth.
Abbreviations: tablespoon – tblsp
                        teaspoon – tsp
(See also Chapters 5 and 6)

Alaska

GIN

ABBEY

medium-sweet – hint of herbs. S.

1½ gin
½ Lillet
1 orange juice
dash of Angostura

Stir with ice. Strain into cocktail-glass. Decorate with cherry on stick.

ADDISON*

medium-dry. S.

1½ gin
1 red vermouth

Shake with ice. Strain into cocktail-glass. Add strip of orange peel.

AGONY*

agreeably bitter-sweet. S.

1½ gin
½ white rum
1 lemon juice
1 tsp sugar

Shake with ice. Strain into cocktail-glass.

ALASKA

a touch of luxury – medium-dry. S.

2 gin
1 yellow Chartreuse
2 dashes Angostura

Shake with ice. Strain into cocktail-glass. Add twist of lemon peel.

BARBARA WEST*

medium-dry. S.

1 gin
1 sweet sherry
½ lemon juice
dash Angostura

Stir with ice. Strain into cocktail-glass.

BEE'S KNEES*

bitter-sweet aftertaste. S.

2 gin
1 clear honey
1 lemon juice

Shake with ice. Strain into cocktail-glass.

BETTY JAMES

medium-dry. S.

1 gin
½ lemon juice
1 tblsp maraschino
dash Angostura

Shake with ice. Strain into cocktail-glass.

BLUE BIRD

sky-blue – bitter-sweet. S.

2 gin
¼ blue curaçao
dash Angostura

Stir with ice. Strain into cocktail-glass. Add twist of lemon peel. Decorate with cherry on stick.

BOSTON CLUB

bitter-sweet. S.

1½ gin
1 lemon juice
¼ red vermouth

Shake with ice. Strain into cocktail-glass. Decorate with cherry on stick.

BRONX*   C

longtime favourite – medium-dry. S.

1 gin
½ dry vermouth
½ red vermouth
1 orange juice

Shake with ice. Strain into cocktail-glass. Decorate with cherry on stick.

BULLDOG*

fruitily sweetish. S.

1 gin
1 lemon juice
1½ cherry brandy

Shake with ice. Strain into cocktail-glass. Decorate with cherry on stick.

Clover Club

LADY CHATTERLEY*

not Mellors's choice! – bitter-sweet. S.

2 gin
1 lemon juice
½ cherry brandy

Shake with ice. Strain into cocktail-glass. Decorate with cherry on stick.

CLOVER CLUB*   C

smoothly sweetish. ML.

1½ gin
½ grenadine
white of 1 egg
1 lemon juice
½ tsp sugar

Shake briskly with ice. Strain into goblet.

Left to right: Collins, Coco-Gin and Fluffy Duck (recipe on page 88)

COCO-GIN*

new – sweet ML.

1½ gin
1 Malibu liqueur
1 lemon juice
½ grenadine

Shake with ice. Strain into large cocktail-glass. Option: frost rim of glass with sugar.

COLLINS*   C

Lemony – medium-sweet. ML.

1½ gin
2 tsp sugar
2 tsp lemon juice

Mix in tumbler. Add ice cubes. Top with soda-water.

(A Collins may be made with any spirit: gin is the traditional one.)

DEPTH CHARGE

aromatically sweet. S.

1 gin
1 red vermouth
¼ Pernod

Stir with ice. Strain into cocktail-glass. Add slice of orange peel.

A LONDON CONTRIBUTION

There are few cocktails that owe anything to British inventiveness. But the family of drinks under the COLLINS title are named after an Englishman. He did not evolve any particular drink. He was a servitor in a West End of London hotel at the beginning of the last century, and it is not clear why his name should have been given to a cocktail that was not formalised until after his day. He was immortalised in a poor bit of anonymous contemporary verse, itself totally unmemorable – and yet John Collins is for ever remembered in the continuing story of cocktails:

> My name is John Collins, head waiter at Limmer's,
> Corner of Conduit Street, Hanover Square.
> My main occupation is filling the brimmers
> For all the young gentlemen frequenters there.

To confuse matters, a Tom Collins made its appearance alongside the John Collins. However, we need not bother with any subtle distinctions from the past, nor with variations like Pierre Collins (made with brandy), Mike Collins (with Irish whiskey) and so on. The simple word Collins suffices to describe a certain type of cocktail.

DRY MARTINI*   C

appetisingly sharp. S.

2 gin
¼ tsp dry vermouth

Stir briskly with ice. Strain into (preferably pre-chilled) cocktail-glass. Add twist of lemon peel, squeezed.

(This is a basic recipe. Older versions include dash of orange bitters. Proportion vermouth to gin is very much for individul taste. Some addicts like lemon peel squeezed over drink, not immersed. Green olive on stick is optional extra. Dry Martinis are often served on-the-rocks: the method given above is called 'straight up'. See panel on page 88 and illustration on page 90.)

DUBONNY*

hint of tartness – medium-dry. S.

1 gin
1 Dubonnet
½ dry vermouth
½ medium-dry sherry
dash Angostura

Stir with ice. Strain into cocktail-glass.

EARTHQUAKE

potentially dangerous – bitter-sweet. S.

1 gin
1 whisky
1 Pernod

Shake with ice. Strain into cocktail-glass.

EMERALD ISLE

sweet. S.

2 gin
½ crème de menthe
2 dashes Angostura

Stir with ice. Strain into cocktail-glass.

FIBBER McGEE* C

we do not lie – it's semi-sweet. S.

2 gin
½ red vermouth
1 grapefruit juice
2 dashes Angostura

Stir with ice. Strain into cocktail-glass.

FLORIDA

cryptically bitter-sweet. ML.

1 gin
2 grapefruit juice
1 Galliano
½ Campari

Shake with ice. Strain into large cocktail-glass. Decorate with half-slice of orange.

FLUFFY DUCK

decidedly sweet. ML.

1 gin
1 advocaat
1 orange juice
½ Cointreau

Pour on-the-rocks in goblet. Stir. Top with soda-water. (Origin: Australia)
See illustration on page 86.

FRENCH KISS

sweet as you'd expect. S.

2 gin
1 Cointreau

Pour on-the-rocks in tumbler. Stir. Add round of orange.

THE MOST FAMOUS

The anecdotes and legends surrounding the DRY MARTINI are legion. It is the only single cocktail to have at least three full-length books (the first British, the others American), devoted entirely to it – and to its many mutations. It is widely thought the name comes from the famous Vermouth: incorrect. Though that brand is now often preferred, there was no Dry Vermouth made by Martini & Rossi when the cocktail first saw glass. Nor, as some aver, does it stem from the very old Martinez cocktail, which was a sweet mix.

The author discovered twenty years ago what is most probably the true, but lost, story of the evolvement of the Dry Martini. The date is about 1910, the place the (since vanished) fashionable Knickerbocker Hotel, New York City. The man was Signor Martini, head bartender. He transformed the well-known gin-and-French by blending the ingredients – gin, Dry Vermouth and orange bitters – with ice, straining into a cocktail glass and adding a twist of lemon peel. We do not know when the once obligatory green olive (less popular today) became an optional garnish. A celebrated early admirer of Signor Martini's invention was the oil tycoon, John D. Rockefeller.

Though its fame has endured – even amongst people who never drink it – the Dry Martini is much less drunk today: it is no longer the Americans' favourite cocktail. Yet, when cocktails are spoken of, it incites more comment than any other.

GIBSON

sharp. S.

(A Dry Martini served with a pearl onion on stick as sole garnish)

GIMLET* C

bitter-sweet. S.

1½ gin
1½ Rose's lime juice cordial
1 tsp lemon juice

Shake with ice. Strain into cocktail-glass.

FROM PROHIBITION DAYS

The GIBSON is a once highly esteemed variant of the classic Dry Martini. It was a child of Prohibition. To avoid its rigours, the Players Club, in New York City – celebrated resort of actors, artists and authors – made over its bar to the bartender, Charley Connolly. He ran it personally as a Speakeasy, exclusively for Players' members, and good, if illicit, alcohol flowed without interference during the whole 'dry' era.

One day, the famous artist Charles Dana Gibson, creator of the Gibson Girl, asked Charley to tempt his jaded palate with a 'better Dry Martini'. Charley made one in the traditional manner, but for garnish he used a pearl onion impaled on a stick. This did, in fact, subtly alter the cocktail's taste, and its visual appeal. Members of the Players started ordering Gibsons. The innovation gradually spread to other superior Speakeasies and private homes and, by the time drinking again became legal – in 1933 – the Gibson had firmly established a separate identity in the repertoire of cocktails.

(Originally made with fresh lime juice, not cordial; it was named, for its sharpness, after the carpenter's tool) *May be served on-the-rocks. ML.*

GIN FIZZ*   C

bitter-sweet. ML.

1 gin
½ tsp lemon juice
1 tsp sugar

Shake with ice. Strain into large cocktail-glass. Add splash of soda-water.

GIN RICKEY

medium-dry. S.

see Rickey

Emerald Isle ▶

GOLD FIZZER

refreshingly sweet. L.

2 gin
1 tsp grenadine syrup
1 tsp sugar
1 lemon juice
yolk of 1 egg

Shake briskly with ice. Strain on-the-rocks into tall glass. Top with good orange squash.

GUNGA DIN

sweetish. S.

2 gin
½ dry vermouth
1 orange juice

Shake with ice. Strain into cocktail-glass. Optional: decorate with cube of pineapple on stick.

INCOME TAX

sweeter than its name. S.

1½ gin
1 orange juice
¼ red vermouth
¼ dry vermouth
dash Angostura

Shake with ice. Strain into cocktail-glass.

JOHN COLLINS

see Collins and Cock-tale: 'A London Contribution'

KNICKERBOCKER

medium-dry. S.

1½ gin
1 dry vermouth
½ red vermouth

Stir with ice. Strain into cocktail-glass.

Dry Martini (recipe on page 87)

LONDONER

sweetish. L.

2 gin
2 rose-hip syrup
1 tsp lemon juice

Pour on to ice cubes in tall glass. Top with soda-water. Add round of orange.

LONDON FOG*

bitter-sweet. ML.

2 gin
1 Pernod

Pour on to crushed ice in goblet. Add a little soda-water. Serve with straws.

MAIDEN'S PRAYER*

appealingly sweet. S.

1 gin
1 Cointreau
½ orange juice
½ lemon juice

Shake. Strain into cocktail-glass of which rim has been frosted with sugar.

MARTINEZ*

sweet. S.

1 gin
1 red vermouth
¼ tsp sugar
dash Angostura

Stir with ice. Strain into cocktail-glass. Decorate with cherry on stick.

MARTINI

see Dry Martini

MICKEY FINN

medium-dry. S.

1 gin
1 dry vermouth
¼ crème de menthe
¼ Pernod

Shake with ice. Strain into cocktail-glass. Decorate with cherry on stick.

NEGRONI   C

delectably bitter-sweet. ML.

1 gin
1 red vermouth
½ Campari

Pour on to ice cubes in goblet. Stir. Top with soda-water. Add round of orange.

NEW YORKER

medium-dry. S.

1 gin
1 dry vermouth
½ medium-dry sherry
1 tsp Cointreau

Stir with ice. Strain into cocktail-glass.

> Quantities are expressed in number(s) or fractions of a measure of 1 fl. oz/25 ml capacity, except where other quantities are stated.

BOGUS COLONEL – GOOD DRINK

A cocktail which deserves revival is the gin RICKEY, though a complication for Britons is that is really does call for a fresh lime: lemon will only just about do instead. It is an honest drink that takes its name from a man of dubious probity. He was Colonel Jim Rickey, a lobbyist in Washington DC around the turn of the century. He was not a colonel, though he may have been one of the Kentucky variety, and his real first name was Joe. Anyway, 'Colonel Jim' did a lot of his business with Congressmen, amongst whom he was popular, in Shoomaker's Bar. It was there, in collusion with the bartender, he dreamed up the mix which alone commemorates him.

ORANGE BLOOM

sweet. S.

2 gin
1 red vermouth
½ Cointreau

Stir with ice. Strain into cocktail-glass. Optional: frost rim of glass with sugar.

PICCADILLY

bitter-sweet. S.

1½ gin
1 dry vermouth
¼ Pernod
½ tsp grenadine

Stir with ice. Strain into cocktail-glass.

RICKEY*   C

deliciously bitter-sweet. ML.

2 gin
1 fresh lime (or lemon) juice
½ tsp grenadine

Pour gin on to ice cubes in tumbler. Add grenadine. Squeeze juice direct from half of lime (small lemon). Put the squeezed fruit into the tumbler. Stir. Top with soda-water.

ROLLS ROYCE

opulently medium-dry. S.

2 gin
1 red vermouth
½ dry vermouth
1 tsp Bénédictine

Shake with ice. Strain into cocktail-glass.

SHEEP DIP

nicer than its title: sweetish. ML.

2 gin
1 dry sherry
3 sweet cider

Shake with ice. Strain into goblet.

SILVER STREAK   C

digestively sweet. S.

1½ gin
½ kummel

Pour on to crushed ice in cocktail-glass. Serve with straws.

TRINITY   C

medium-dry. S.

1 gin
1 red vermouth
1 dry vermouth

Stir with ice. Strain into cocktail-glass. Decorate with cherry on stick.

(This is sometimes listed under the title Perfect or Ideal, which is very much a matter of opinion).

WHITE LADY*   C

beautifully bitter-sweet. S.

1 gin
½ lemon juice
½ Cointreau
1 tsp egg white

Shake briskly with ice. Strain into cocktail-glass.

Silver Streak

Left to right: Black Russian, Blue Lagoon and Balalaika

Today it is considered quite correct to use vodka in place of gin for virtually all cocktails traditionally associated with the latter. They will not be exactly the same: gin has more character than vodka.

It does not follow that gin is a satisfactory alternative to vodka in mixes specifically evolved for the newer spirit.

VODKA

BALALAIKA*

bitter-sweet. S.

1 vodka
1 lemon juice
½ Cointreau

Shake with ice. Strain into cocktail-glass.

BLACKRUSSIAN   C

coffee's mate: sweet. ML.

1½ vodka
1 Kahlua

Mix on-the-rocks in tumbler.

(Tia Maria may replace Kahlua; use marginally more.)

BLUE LAGOON

the sweet blue sea. ML.

1 vodka
1 blue curaçao

Pour on-the-rocks in goblet. Top with fizzy lemonade.

THANK YOU, 'SANK'

In central Paris, in narrow rue Danou, is Harry's New York Bar, scarcely changed since the day it opened at No. 5 in 1911. For the benefit of monolinguistic visitors, its card phonetically gives the address as 'sank roo doe noo'. It was in the 1920s a favoured social centre for expatriates, American in particular – Hemingway and his ilk, and more especially those who thought they were like Hemingway. It became one of the few celebrated cocktail bars of the world, though in no way a smart place. It was dedicated to serious drinking – and talk. In 1924, the International Bar Flies club was founded in Harry's.

It is claimed that three Cocktails of lasting value were evolved in rue Danou. The first, the elegant WHITE LADY, is appropriately named. The second, the SIDE-CAR, allegedly derives from the fact that the unknown toper for whom it was invented used to arrive at the bar in the sidecar of a motor-cycle, in the twenties a common form of urban transport.

However, the bar's most important contribution, in terms of modern drinking, was the conception of the BLOODY MARY, today arguably the single most popular cocktail (in its sundry forms). It was first made, in those fabulous twenties, by Fernand Petiot, a bartender at Harry's.

Harry's clientele has changed: it is now less a tourist attraction, has a less aggressively masculine ambience, and is considered a *chic* meeting-place by some young French business executives. But we owe it a nostalgic vote of thanks for those three cocktails.

BLOODY MARY*   C

with savoury tang. ML./L.

2 vodka
5 tomato juice
1 tsp Worcester sauce & lemon juice
dash of salt, celery salt, cayenne pepper, Tabasco

Mix thoroughly on-the-rocks in goblet. Optional: serve with short stick of celery as edible stirrer.

(There are umpteen versions of this drink. Originally a short cocktail, it has become usual to serve it as a fairly substantial one. Number and proportion of condiments is for personal discretion).

BULLSHOT   C

meaty zing. ML./L.

Made as a Bloody Mary, substituting condensed canned consommé for tomato juice.

A combination of consommé and tomato juice produces a Bloody Bullshot.

a zestful compromise. ML./L.

Bloody Mary

Left to right: Moscow Mule,
Old Smoothie and Muscovital

HARVEY WALLBANGER   C

provokingly sweet. ML.

2 vodka

Pour on-the-rocks into goblet. Top with orange juice. Float on top
1 Galliano.

HEADLESS HORSEMAN*

medium-dry. L.

2 vodka
2 dashes Angostura

Pour on to several ice cubes in tall glass. Add round of orange. Top with ginger ale.

MARLBOROUGH*

dreamily sweet. S.

1 vodka
1 Bailey's Irish Cream
½ orange juice

Shake with ice. Strain into cocktail-glass. Serve with cherry on stick.

MOSCOW MULE*   C

exhilaratingly bitter-sweet. L.

1½ vodka
½ fresh lime (or lemon) juice

Pour on-the-rocks into tall glass. Fill with ginger beer.

MUSCOVITAL

vitalisingly bitter-sweet. S.

1 vodka
1 Campari
2 ginger wine

Mix with ice in tumbler. Decorate with cherry on stick.

OLD SMOOTHIE

medium-dry. ML.

1½ vodka
1 Galliano
½ lemon juice

Shake with ice. Strain into large cocktail-glass half-filled with crushed ice. Serve with straws.

SCREWDRIVER*   C

deliciously sweet. ML.

2 vodka

Pour on to ice cubes in tumbler. Top with orange juice.

TWISTER*

bitter-sweet. ML.

2 vodka

Pour over ice cubes in goblet. Squeeze juice from half a small lemon and add the squeezed fruit to the drink. Top with 7-Up or fizzy lemonade.

VODKATINI

decidedly dry. S.

A Dry Martini (see Gin) made with vodka. In the author's opinion this is improved if very slightly more dry vermouth is used than in the traditional version. Also, a twist of grapefruit peel rather than lemon gives a Vodkatini individuality.

YELLOW FEVER

sharp. L.

In tall glass, dissolve ½ tsp sugar in a little vodka. Add
1 lemon juice, and stir
2 vodka, stir again, adding ice cubes.
Top with soda-water.
Decorate with round of orange.

WHITE RUM

ACAPULCO

sweet. S.

1 white rum
½ fresh lime (or lemon) juice
2 tsp Cointreau
1 tsp egg white
½ tsp sugar

Shake with ice. Strain into cocktail-glass. Decorate with small mint sprig in season.

BACARDI COCKTAIL   C

Daiquiri (see below) made only with Bacardi rum.

BOSTON COOLER

medium-dry. L.

2 white rum
1 lemon juice
1 tsp sugar

Dissolve sugar in lemon juice in tall glass. Add ice cubes. Fill with ginger ale. Add twist of orange peel.

Quantities are expressed in number(s) or fractions of a measure of 1 fl. oz/25 ml capacity, except where other quantities are stated.

CUBA LIBRE*   C

medium-sweet. L.

1½ white rum
1 tsp lemon juice

Pour on-the-rocks in tall glass. Top with Coca-Cola.

DAIQUIRI   C

superbly bitter-sweet. S.

1 white rum
1 fresh lime (or lemon) juice
½ grenadine syrup

Shake briskly with ice until very cold. Strain into cocktail-glass.

(Cointreau may be substituted for grenadine. Other fruit syrups are also used in place of – or in addition to – grenadine. Strawberry is a popular flavour. The Daiquiri has achieved a large number of versions. Frozen Daiquiris are made by combining ingredients – for several servings – with crushed ice in electric blender)

HAVANA*

bitter-sweet. S.

1 white rum
1 cream sherry
½ tsp lemon juice

Shake with ice. Strain into cocktail-glass.

◄ **Cuba Libre**

THE CUBAN CONNECTION

When it comes to the DAIQUIRI, which has enjoyed enormous popularity (often in mutated form) in the USA in recent years, you have a choice of legends.

First: in the early days of the century, when Cuba had gained independence, some American engineers were working at the Daiquiri nickel mine in Oriente province. They ran out of imported Whiskey. Their steward made up a drink with white rum, cane-sugar syrup and fresh lime juice, all items in copious local supply. The men found it delicious and named the drink after their place of employment.

Second: from approximately the same period, the Spanish-American War (1898) which freed Cuba. Admiral Lucius Johnson effected a landing in Cuba on Daiquiri beach. Seeking refreshing beverage for his men he discovered the native Cubans were drinking an equivalent of the mix we now call by the name of that stretch of sand. He took a written recipe to the Army and Navy Club in Washington, D.C., where it is part of the club's archives.

There is a further Cuban connection – through CUBA LIBRE. This was popularised during Prohibition when Americans who could afford to hopped over from nearby Florida to Havana. The name was a bit of a joke – Cuba the Free – for Cuba was then under despotic rule, if one of a different complexion to that now governing.

HAVANA BEACH

our sweet own. L.

2 white rum
1 orange juice
1 cherry brandy

Pour over ice cubes in tall glass. Stir. Top with Coca-Cola. Add round of orange.

HOLLYWOOD

1½ white rum
½ grapefruit juice
½ grenadine syrup
2 tsp egg white

Shake briskly with ice. Strain into cocktail-glass. Optional: sprinkle on top a little powdered nutmeg.

MARY PICKFORD

sweet as the World's Sweetheart. S.

2 white rum
1 pineapple juice
1 tsp grenadine syrup
1 tsp maraschino

Shake with ice. Strain into cocktail-glass. Decorate with cherry on stick. See illustration on page 115.

PIÑA COLADA   C

sweetish favourite. L.

2 white rum
2 Malibu
2 pineapple juice

Blend or shake well with ice. Strain into tall glass half-filled with crushed ice. Decorate with pineapple cubes on stick. Serve with straws.

THIRD RAIL

medium-dry. S.

1½ white rum
½ red vermouth
½ dry vermouth
1 orange juice

Shake with ice. Strain into cocktail-glass.

TEQUILA

BLOODY MARIA

piquantly sharp. ML.

A Bloody Mary (see Vodka) made with tequila. Frost rim of glass with salt. Also known as the Sangre.

CHARLEY GOODLEG

sweet. L.

2 tequila
1 Galliano

Shake with ice. Strain on-the-rocks into tall glass (of which rim frosted with sugar). Top with orange juice. Stir.

COCOTEQ

a sweet Original. S.

1 tequila
½ Malibu
½ lemon juice
1 tsp grenadine syrup (or
    maraschino)

Shake with ice. Strain into cocktail-glass. Optional: frost rim of glass with sugar. See illustration on page 100.

EL DIABLO

sweetish. L.

1 tequila
½ blackcurrant syrup
½ lemon juice

Shake with ice. Strain on-the-rocks into tall glass. Top with ginger ale.

EXORCIST

bitter-sweet. S.

1½ tequila
1 lemon juice
1 blue curaçao

Shake with ice. Strain into cocktail-glass (of which rim frosted with salt).

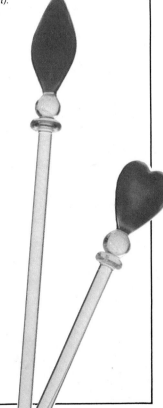

Left to right: Cocoteq (recipe on page 99), Macho and Margarita

FREDDY FUDPUCKER

delightfully sweet. L.

Pour 2 tequila on-the-rocks in tall glass. Top with orange juice. Float on top 1 Galliano. Do not stir.

MACHO

differently dry. ML.

1 tequila
1 Pernod

Pour into large cocktail-glass with lots of crushed ice. Stir. Add
1 tsp lemon juice
Serve with straws

MARGARITA*   C

oddly bitter-sweet. S.

1½ tequila
1 fresh lime (or lemon) juice
½ Cointreau.

*Shake briskly. Strain into cocktail-
glass of which rim frosted with salt.
See panel on page 102.*

MEXICAN ROSE

medium-sweet. S.

2 tequila
1 lemon juice
1 blackcurrant syrup (or crème de
    Cassis)

*Shake with ice. Strain into cocktail-
glass.*

SUNSET

sharply-sugary. S.

2 tequila
1 lemon juice
1 grenadine syrup

*Shake with ice. Strain into cocktail-
glass of which rim frosted with salt.
Decorate with twist of lemon peel.*

(For better-known Sunrise, see
Cream Cocktails.)

Freddy Fudpucker

A SAD CASE OF 'LEAD-POISONING'

In the old Wild West of the USA, in Virginia City, two drinkers fell to arguing. As was not unusual they went into the street and started to settle their dispute with Colt six-shooter 'Peacemakers'. As the bullets flew wildly, a girl of the town was caught in the hail of lead. Her boy-friend, a Mexican bartender, rushed out of the saloon: she died in his arms. Later, he made up a drink based on the Tequila they used to share and he named it after his lost love. Her name was MARGARITA (page 101).

TEQUILA CALIENTE

medium-dry. ML.

2 tequila
1 blackcurrant syrup
1 lemon juice
½ tsp maraschino

Shake with ice. Strain into large cocktail-glass. Add splash of soda-water.

TEQUINI

tart. S.

2 tequila
½ dry vermouth

Stir with ice. Strain into cocktail-glass. Decorate with green olive on stick.

SCOTCH WHISKY

AFFINITY*

medium-dry. S.

1 Scotch
½ dry vermouth
½ red vermouth
2 dashes Angostura

Stir with ice. Strain into cocktail-glass. Decorate with cherry on stick.

ATHOLL BROSE

sweet. ML.

2 Scotch
1 cream
1 clear honey

Mix in warmed glass. Cool in refrigerator. No ice.

BENEDICT ARNOLD

treacherously sweet. S.

2 Scotch
½ Bénédictine

Mix on-the-rocks in small tumbler.

BLOOD & SAND   C

sweetish. S.

1 Scotch
1 orange juice
½ red vermouth
½ cherry brandy

Shake with ice. Strain into cocktail-glass.

BOBBY BURNS   C

sweet. S.

1 Scotch
1 red vermouth
1 tsp Drambuie

Stir with ice. Strain into cocktail-glass.

CHURCHILL*

medium-dry. S.

1½ Scotch
½ red vermouth
½ Cointreau
1 tsp lemon juice

Shake with ice. Strain into cocktail-glass.

FLYING SCOTSMAN*

medium-dry. S.

1 Scotch
1 red vermouth
¼ tsp sugar
dash Angostura

Stir with ice. Strain into cocktail-glass.

GENTLE JOHN*

medium-dry. S.

2 Scotch
1 dry vermouth
¼ Cointreau
dash of Angostura

Stir with ice. Strain into cocktail-glass.

HARRY LAUDER*

spiritedly sweet. S.

1½ Scotch
1½ red vermouth
½ tsp sugar

Shake with ice. Strain into cocktail-glass.

Quantities are expressed in number(s) or fractions of a measure of 1 fl. oz/25 ml capacity, except where other quantities are stated.

HOLE-IN-ONE

sharp. S.

2 Scotch
1 dry vermouth
½ lemon juice
dash of orange bitters

Stir with ice. Strain into cocktail-glass.

LOCH LOMOND*

medium-dry. S.

2 Scotch
½ tsp sugar
3 dashes Angostura

Stir with ice. Strain into cocktail-glass.

PRINCE EDWARD

sweet. S.

2 Scotch
½ Lillet
½ Drambuie

Stir with ice. Strain into cocktail-glass. Add half-slice of orange.

ROBERT BURNS

aniseed-sugary. S.

2 Scotch
½ red vermouth
1 tsp Pernod

Stir with ice. Strain into cocktail-glass.

Left to right: Whisky Sour (recipe on page 104), Lock Lomand and Blood and Sand

Rob Roy

WHISKY SOUR* C

stimulatingly medium-dry. S./ML.

1 Scotch
1½ lemon juice
½ tsp sugar
1 tsp egg white

Shake briskly with ice. Strain into cocktail-glass. Or omit egg white; strain into large cocktail-glass and top with soda-water. See illustration on page 103.

It would be unusual to employ any whisky other than Scotch for the above-mentioned mixes. However, except in the instance of Classics, Scotch can be satisfactorily used for the cocktails in the next section.

OTHER WHISK(E)Y COCKTAILS

We indicate the type associated with the recipe, but its use is not essential.

ADMIRAL*

sharp. S.

1½ Bourbon
½ dry vermouth
½ lemon juice

Shake with ice. Strain into cocktail-glass.

ADMIRAL'S HIGHBALL

medium-dry. L.

1 Bourbon
1 sweet white wine
1 tsp pineapple juice
½ tsp lemon juice

Mix on-the-rocks in tall glass. Top with soda-water.

ROB ROY* C

medium-sweet. S.

2 Scotch
1 red vermouth

Stir with ice. Strain into cocktail-glass.

RUSTY NAIL C

(See Chapter 9.)

STONE FENCE*

refreshingly medium-dry. L.

2 Scotch
¼ tsp sugar
2 dashes Angostura

Mix on-the-rocks in tall glass. Top with medium-dry cider. Decorate with twist of orange peel.

WHISKY MAC* C

(See Chapter 9.)

ALGONQUIN
dry-ish. S.

1½ Bourbon
1 dry vermouth
1 pineapple juice

Shake with ice. Strain into cocktail-glass.

BOILERMAKER
defies comment! L.

1½ Bourbon poured over ice cubes in tall glass. Top with light beer.

BRAINSTORM
medium-dry. ML.

2 Irish whiskey
1 tsp dry vermouth
½ tsp Bénédictine

Mix on-the-rocks in tumbler. Add twist of lemon peel.

Quantities are expressed in number(s) or fractions of a measure of 1 fl. oz/25 ml capacity, except where other quantities are stated.

BROOKLYN
dry. S.

1 Bourbon
1 dry vermouth
¼ maraschino
¼ Amer Picon

Stir with ice. Strain into cocktail-glass.

BUCKAROO*
medium-sweet. L.

2 Bourbon
3 dashes Angostura

Mix on-the-rocks in tall glass. Top with Coca-Cola.

DRINK UP – FAST!

The term HIGHBALL is essentially American, and a little dated at that, familiar to the rest of the world through books and films. It is an odd term for a drink and, for a change, the reason is well documented.

On American railroads, in their early days, a ball suspended from a mast was used to give instructions to drivers of locomotives passing through a station. If the ball was hauled to the top, known therefore as a 'high ball', it signalled to the railman that he should put on steam. The connection between speed and drinking was first made in St. Louis, where a High-Ball was used locally for a simple drink of spirits which could be made and downed quickly. Duly, the word passed into the nation's language, remaining long after 'high balls' had been superseded by more effective forms of railroad communications.

BUNNY HUG
peculiar, sweet. S.

1 Bourbon
1 Pernod
1 gin

Stir with ice. Strain into cocktail-glass

(Be wary of having a second one!)

CANADIAN CHERRY
medium-dry. ML.

2 Canadian whisky
1 Cherry Heering (or cherry brandy)
1 tsp lemon juice
1 tsp orange juice

Shake with ice. Strain into large cocktail-glass. Optional: frost rim of glass with sugar.

CAPETOWN
medium-dry. S.

2 Bourbon
1 Dubonnet
¼ tsp Cointreau
dash Angostura

Stir with ice. Strain into cocktail-glass.

CHEERS
sweet. S.

2 Bourbon
1 Cointreau
1 tsp marashino

Stir with ice. Strain into cocktail-glass.

DALLAS

like TV, medium-sweet. L.

2 Bourbon
1 Southern Comfort
½ lemon juice
½ grenadine syrup

Pour on to ice cubes in tall glass. Stir. Top with soda-water. Decorate with cherries on stick and slice of lemon. Serve with straws.

DIZZY

medium-dry. S.

1 Bourbon
1 medium sherry
½ lemon juice
½ pineapple juice

Shake with ice. Strain into cocktail-glass.

FUN IN BED

as a cynic says — medium-sweet. S.

2 Bourbon
2 grape juice

Shake with ice. Strain into cocktail-glass of which rim has been frosted in sugar.

GLOOM-LIFTER

medium-dry. M.L.

1½ Irish whiskey
1 lemon juice
¼ brandy
½ grenadine syrup
½ tsp sugar
1 tsp egg white

Shake briskly with ice. Strain into large cocktail-glass.

GODFATHER

sweeter than the Mafia. M.L.

2 Bourbon
½ Amaretto

Mix on-the-rocks in tumbler. Decorate with cherry on stick.

GREEN-EYED MONSTER

but he's sweet. S.

2 Irish whiskey
1 red vermouth
½ crème de menthe
dash Angostura

Stir with ice. Strain into cocktail-glass.

HARI-KARI*

a medium-dry nip: M.L.

2 Bourbon
1 tsp sugar
1 lemon juice

Shake with ice. Strain into goblet. Top with soda-water.

LIBERAL   C

bitter-sweet. S.

1 Canadian whisky
1 red vermouth
½ tsp Amer Picon

Stir with ice. Strain into cocktail-glass. Add twist of orange peel.

LOS ANGELES*

medium-dry. M.L.

1½ Bourbon
1 lemon juice
½ red vermouth
1 tsp sugar
1 egg

Shake briskly with ice. Strain into cocktail-glass.

MANHATTAN*   C

traditionally, medium-sweet. S.

1 Bourbon
½ red vermouth
½ dry vermouth
dash Angostura

Stir with ice. Strain into cocktail-glass. Add cherry on stick.
See panel on page 108.

Left to right: Manhattan, Old Fashioned (recipe on page 108) and Godfather

MINT JULEP   C

a drink apart. L.

2 Bourbon (and only Bourbon)
4 sprigs fresh mint
1 lump sugar
1 tblsp water

Crush mint, sugar and water in tall glass. Nearly fill glass with ice. Pour in the Bourbon. Do not stir. Garnish with fresh mint.

(There have, inevitably, been many versions of this essential American mix, famous – but little drunk – outside the U.S.A. This is virtually an 'official' recipe.)

OLD FASHIONED*   C

medium-dry. M.L.

2 Bourbon (or other American
    whiskey)
1 tsp sugar
3 dashes Angostura

Stir in tumbler with ice cubes. Add slice of orange and cocktail cherry. See illustration on page 106.

QUEBEC

medium-dry. S.

1½ Canadian whisky
½ dry vermouth
½ maraschino
1 tsp Amer Picon

Stir with ice. Strain into cocktail-glass.

RABBIT'S REVENGE

sweet. M.L.

2 Bourbon
2 pineapple juice
1 tsp maraschino

Shake with ice. Strain on-the-rocks into goblet. Top with ginger ale. Decorate with round of orange.

SERPENT'S TOOTH   C

medium-sweet. M.L.

1½ Irish whiskey
2 red vermouth
1 lemon juice
½ kümmel
dash Angostura

Shake with ice. Strain into large cocktail-glass.

SNOOPY

medium-dry. M.L.

1½ Bourbon
1 Galliano
1 Campari
½ Cointreau
½ tsp lemon juice

Shake with ice. Strain into large cocktail-glass. Add twist of lemon peel.

TEMPTATION

almost as sweet as sin. S.

2 Bourbon
¼ Pernod
¼ Dubonnet
¼ Cointreau

Shake with ice. Strain into cocktail-glass.

TENNESSEE

medium-dry. S.

1½ Tennessee sour mash whiskey
    (Jack Daniel's)
½ lemon juice
½ maraschino

Shake with ice. Strain into cocktail-glass. Decorate with cherry on stick.

AMERICAN DUO

The OLD FASHIONED is an enduring American cocktail which first appeared at the chic Pendennis Club in Louisville, Kentucky, around a century ago. During Prohibition it was easily adapted to bad illegal hooch by putting extra fruit into it. The mix survived the dread period of drought and, after Repeal, resumed its original style.

One would think the MANHATTAN, long one of the USA's premier Cocktails, was obviously a product of that most fasionable area, rich in smart bars. It only belongs to Manhatten by adoption. It derives from a mix originally concocted hurriedly in Maryland, in 1846, to revive a man wounded in a duel. We are not told if he recovered, but the drink was found stimulating by the uninjured, and was somewhat improved on when it reached New York City. (Recipe on page 107.)

ARABY IN THE DEEP SOUTH

Though not often made outside the USA, the MINT JULEP is famous through countless novels and movies dealing with the Deep South. This is the drink that instantly conjures up a snowy-haired old Black butler carrying, on a silver tray, a frost-beaded glass of Julep to a distinguished Kentucky colonel sitting on the broad porch of his splendid Colonial mansion, as, across the lawn, Southern belles flirt with young officers . . . or something like that.

But why that strange word Julep? It is of ancient Arabic origin. The Moorish physicians of centuries past concocted pleasant sweet liquids, *julab*, that they used to disguise the obnoxious taste of medicinal herbal compounds. Persian doctors used similarly-named mixtures: rose-water was an ingredient.

How and when this term arrived in the USA and why it became applied to a delicious spirituous beverage – abhorrent to Islam – we do not know. The only connection is a Middle East delight in mint.

BRANDY

It is, of course, preferable to use a good standard grade of Cognac, such as Hennessy Three Star, but a quality 'grape brandy' (see the Brandy section of Chapter 1) will adequately fill the bill – and also reduce the bill.

ANTONIO
medium-dry. S.

1 brandy
1 gin
¼ crème de menthe
¼ maraschino

Shake with ice. Strain into cocktail-glass.

BARNEY BARNATO
sweet. S.

1 brandy
1 Dubonnet
½ Cointreau
dash Angostura

Stir with ice. Strain into cocktail-glass.

BENNY
medium-dry. S.

2 brandy
1 Bénédictine
½ lemon juice
2 dashes Angostura

Shake with ice. Strain into cocktail-glass. Optional: frost rim of glass with sugar.

BETSY ROSS*   C
sweetly unusual. S.

1 brandy
1 port
¼ Cointreau
dash Angostura

Stir with ice. Strain into cocktail-glass.

BETWEEN THE SHEETS   C
medium-dry. S.

1 brandy
1 lemon juice
½ white run
1 Cointreau

Shake with ice. Strain into cocktail-glass.

BOMBAY
sweet. S.

2 brandy
¼ dry vermouth
¼ red vermouth
¼ tsp Cointreau
¼ tsp Pernod

Stir with ice. Strain into cocktail-glass.

BONANZA*
medium-sweet. L.

1 brandy
1 medium sherry

Pour on-the-rocks in tall glass. Top with 'Hock' style white wine.

BONNIE PRINCE CHARLIE   C
bitter-sweet. S.

1 brandy
½ Drambuie
1 lemon juice

Shake with ice. Strain into cocktail-glass

BOOSTER*   C

medium-dry. S.

2 brandy
½ Cointreau
1 tsp egg white

Shake briskly with ice. Strain into cocktail-glass. Optional: dust a little powdered nutmeg on top.

BRANDY ALEXANDER*   C

(See Cream Cocktails.)

BRANDY CASSIS

medium-sweet. S.

2 brandy
½ lemon juice
1 blackcurrant syrup (or crème de Cassis)

Shake with ice. Strain into cocktail-glass.

BUMBLE BEE

medium-dry. S.

1½ brandy
1 Galliano
½ Pernod

Shake with ice. Strain into cocktail-glass.

CHERRY BLOSSOM

sweetish. M.L.

1 brandy
1 cherry brandy
1 lemon
½ Cointreau
½ grenadine syrup

Shake with ice. Strain into large cocktail-glass.

CHICAGO*

medium-dry. S.

2 brandy
½ Cointreau
2 dashes Angostura

Stir with ice. Strain into cocktail-glass.

DIRTY DOG

refreshingly sweet. L.

2 brandy
1 Tia Maria

Pour on-the-rocks in tall glass. Fill with grapefruit juice.

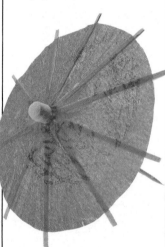

DON'T GO NEAR THE WATER

medium-sweet. S.

2 brandy
½ lemon juice
¼ Cointreau
¼ maraschino (or grenadine syrup)

Shake with ice. Strain into cocktail-glass. Optional: frost rim of glass with sugar.

DREAM

medium-sweet. S.

1½ brandy
1 Cointreau
¼ Pernod

Shake with ice. Strain into cocktail-glass.

EPÉE   C

lightly aromatic; sweetish. S.

2 brandy
½ red vermouth
dash Angostura
Stir with ice. Strain into cocktail-glass.

GEORGIA BEAUTY

smoothly dry-ish. L.

2 brandy
1 lemon juice
2 tsp sugar
1 egg

Shake with ice. Strain on-the-rocks into tall glass. Stir. Top with soda-water.

GOLD COCONUT*

new combination; excitingly semi-sweet. M.L.

1 brandy
1 Malibu
2 orange juice
1 tsp egg white
dash of grenadine syrup

Shake briskly with ice. Strain on-the-rocks into tumbler. Decorate with cherry and small slice of orange on stick.

Send your own cocktail recipes to us at Peter Dominic's Wine Mine Club, Vintner House, River Way, Harlow, Essex. (See page 152).

GRANADA*

medium-dry. M.L.

1 brandy
1 dry sherry
½ Cointreau

Shake with ice. Strain into goblet. Top with tonic-water.

GRENADIER*

gingery, sweetish. S.

2 brandy
2 ginger wine
½ tsp sugar

Shake with ice. Strain into cocktail-glass.

HELL

the reality can't be so sweet. S.

1½ brandy
½ crème de menthe

Mix on-the-rocks in small tumbler. Shake a little cayenne pepper on top.

HORSE'S NECK

medium-dry winner. L.

Hang a spiral of lemon peel inside
    tall glass, suspended from the
    rim.
Add ice cubes
Pour in 2 brandy
dash Angostura
Fill with ginger ale

(This may be made with any spirit. See illustration on page 113.)

ITCHY BITCHY

but no complaints on its strength. S.

1 brandy
½ vodka
½ Cointreau

Mix on-the-rocks in small tumbler.

KISS THE BOYS GOODBYE

with almost dry eyes. S.

1 brandy
½ sloe gin
1 lemon juice
1 tsp egg white

Shake with ice. Strain into cocktail-glass.

◀ **Kiss the Boys Goodbye**

LAST RESORT

serenely sweetish. S.

1 brandy
1 port
½ tsp sugar
1 egg yolk

Shake with ice. Strain into cocktail-glass. Sprinkle powdered nutmeg on top.

SIDECAR*   C

lasting 'twenties favourite: dri-ish. S.

1 brandy
½ lemon juice
½ Cointreau

Shake with ice. Strain into cocktail-glass.

SLOPPY JOE

spells a neat medium-dry drink. M.L.

1 brandy
1 pineapple juice
1 port
¼ Cointreau
½ tsp grenadine syrup

Shake with ice. Strain into large cocktail-glass.

(There are umpteen different Sloppy Joes.)

SNIFTER

on the sweet side. S.

1 brandy
1 Galliano
¼ crème de menthe

Stir with ice. Strain into cocktail-glass.

SUN

brilliantly sweetish. M.L.

2 brandy
½ each of Cointreau, maraschino, lemon juice, pineapple juice
dash Angostura

Shake with ice. Strain on-the-rocks in a goblet.

TIGER'S MILK

semi-sweet. S.

1½ brandy
1½ sloe gin

Shake with ice. Strain into cocktail-glass. Add twist of lemon peel.

Left to right: Brandy Alexander (recipe on page 117), Horse's Neck (page 111) and Sidecar

WEEP NO MORE

fairly sweet. S.

1 brandy
1 Dubonnet
½ grenadine syrup
½ lemon juice

Shake with ice. Strain into cocktail-glass.

YES & NO

make your mind up, sweetly. S.

2 brandy
white of 1 egg
½ Cointreau

Shake briskly with ice. Strain into cocktail-glass. Sprinkle powdered nutmeg on top.

DARK RUM

To a considerable extent, rum recipes can be used with either white or coloured. Unless very pungent rum is preferred, it is suggested that for iced drinks the Navy style should not be used where dark rum is specified, but a somewhat more lightly-flavoured variety. 'Dark' rum is often more golden than inky.

BOLERO

medium-dry. S.

1 dark rum
½ calvados
½ red vermouth

Shake with ice. Strain into cocktail-glass. Add twist of lemon peel.

113

BROADMOOR

strong on flavour: sweetish. L.

2 dark rum
½ crème de menthe
1 lemon juice

Pour on-the-rocks in tall glass. Top with fizzy lemonade or 7-Up.

BUSTER

not for kids: medium-dry. S.

2 dark rum
½ Pernod

Stir with ice. Strain into cocktail-glass. Add half round of lemon.

CLOAK & DAGGER*

no secret – it's pleasantly sweet. L.

1½ dark rum
2 tsp orange juice

Pour on-the-rocks in tall glass. Top with Coca-Cola.

COCONUTTY

a new one: fairly sweet. S.

2 dark rum
2 Malibu
1 lemon juice
1 tsp sugar

Shake with ice. Strain into large cocktail-glass.

DUNLOP*

fairly dry. S.

1 dark rum
1 dry sherry
dash Angostura

Shake with ice. Strain into cocktail-glass.

EL PRESIDENTE

sweetly powerful. S.

2 dark rum
¼ Cointreau
¼ dry vermouth
½ tsp grenadine syrup

Stir with ice. Strain into cocktail-glass.

Left to right: Planter's Punch (recipe on page 116), Mary Pickford (page 99) and Coconutty.

JAMAICAN GLORY*

welcome newcomer: semi-sweet. M.L.

1 dark rum
1 Bailey's Irish Cream
2 lemon juice
½ tsp sugar

Shake with ice. Strain into large cocktail-glass.

MAI TAI

exotically refreshing: fruitily sweet. L.

1 dark rum
2 pineapple juice
2 orange juice
1 lemon juice

Shake well with crushed ice. Pour entire into tall glass. Decorate with pineapple cubes and cherries on stick, and slice of orange. Serve with straws.

PLANTER'S PUNCH*   C

bitter-sweet. M.L.

2 dark rum
½ lemon juice
½ tsp sugar
dash Angostura

Shake with ice. Strain on-the-rocks in goblet. Decorate with fruit in season.

(There are a great many variations on this famous theme. This is a basic recipe. We deal with the drink at more length in next chapter (8). See illustration on page 114.)

CREAM COCKTAILS

Creamy cocktails have become extremely popular in Britain – perhaps partly due to the growth in sales of cream liqueurs. A prime example has been the sensational growth of Bailey's Irish Cream. It is notable that a very high proportion of prize-winning recipes in professional cocktail competitions latterly have contained cream, milk or ice cream.

ACE*

medium-sweet. S.

1 cream
1 tblsp egg white
½ grenadine syrup
1 gin

Shake briskly with ice. Strain into cocktail-glass. Sprinkle powdered nutmeg on top.

ALEXANDRA*

one of ours: sweetish. S.

1 cream
1 Bailey's Irish Cream
1 brandy
½ tsp sugar

Shake with ice. Strain into cocktail-glass. Sprinkle powdered nutmeg on top.

ANGEL'S LIPS

simply, medium-sweet. S.

2 cream
2 Bénédictine

Shake with ice. Strain into cocktail-glass. Decorate with cherry on stick.

APOLLO

slightly exotic: sweet. S.

1 Galliano
½ tequila
½ blue curaçao

Shake with ice. Strain into cocktail-glass. Float cream on top to almost full.

BALTIMORE

worth the trouble: medium-dry. L.

3 milk
1 egg
1 tsp sugar
1 brandy
1 dark rum
1 medium sherry

Shake with ice. Strain into tall glass with crushed ice. Serve with straws. Optional: powdered nutmeg on top.

BANANA COW

richly sweet. L.

5 milk
half a small ripe banana, mashed
1 tsp sugar
2 dark rum

Shake briskly, or blend, with crushed ice. Pour entire into tall glass. Serve with straws.

BARBRA*

our own: sweetish. S.

1 cream
1 Bailey's Irish Cream
1 vodka
½ tsp sugar

Shake briskly with ice. Strain into cocktail-glass with its rim frosted with sugar.

Barbra

BRANDY ALEXANDER   C

veteran favourite with ladies:
sweetish. S.

1 cream
1 brandy
1 crème de cacao

Shake briskly with ice. Strain into
cocktail-glass.
See illustration on page 112.

BRANDY FLIP*   C

smooth: dry-ish. S.

1 cream
1 egg
½ tsp sugar
1 brandy

Shake briskly with ice. Strain into
cocktail-glass. Shake a little
powdered nutmeg on top.

BRANDY ZOOM

smooth, strong, sweet. S.

1 cream
1 tsp clear honey
2 brandy

Shake briskly with ice. Strain into
cocktail-glass.

CAFE ITALIANO

sharpish – or sweet as you like.
M.L.

1 cream
1 strong black coffee
1 Galliano
1 brandy
1 tsp brown sugar

Shake briskly with ice. Strain into
large cocktail-glass.

CHERRY RUM

semi-sweet. S.

1 cream
1 white rum
1 cherry brandy

Shake with ice. Strain into cocktail-
glass.

CONNOISSEUR*

a soft and sweet one of ours. M.L.

2 tblsp soft vanilla ice cream
1 milk
2 Malibu
1 tsp lemon juice

Shake (or blend) briskly with ice.
Strain into goblet.

Quantities are
expressed in
number(s) or fractions of a
measure of 1 fl. oz/25 ml
capacity, except where
other quantities are stated.

CREAM PUFF*

strong, smooth and medium-dry. M.L.

2 cream
2 dark rum
½ tsp sugar

Shake with ice. Strain into goblet on-the-rocks. Top with soda-water.

DINNER-TIME

new: lusciously sweetish. M.L.

2 cream
1 Bailey's Irish Cream
1 whisky

Shake with ice. Strain into large cocktail-glass. Optional: grate a little plain chocolate on top.

PETER'S GRASSHOPPER*

variation on old theme: sweetish. S.

2 cream
1½ Bailey's Irish Cream
1 crème de menthe

Shake well with ice. Strain into cocktail-glass.

FIFTH AVENUE

smartly medium-sweet. M.L.

1 cream
1 Tia Maria
1 brandy
½ tsp sugar

Shake with ice. Strain into cocktail-glass.

GOLDEN CADILLAC   C

Americans' delight: sweet. M.L.

2 cream
1 Tia Maria
1 Galliano

Shake briskly with ice. Strain into large cocktail-glass.

MALIBU ICEBERG*

refreshing: very mildly alcoholic. L.

2 Malibu

Pour over several ice cubes in tall glass. Top with chilled milk. Sprinkle a little powdered nutmeg on top.

Malibu Iceberg

PINK LADY*

a frothy medium-sweet bit. S.

1 cream
1 tsp egg white
1 gin
½ grenadine syrup

Shake with ice. Strain into cocktail-glass with frosted rim.

PLATINUM BLONDE*

'The Monroe Doctrine': medium-sweet. S.

2 cream
2 white rum
1 Cointreau

Shake with ice. Strain into cocktail-glass.

PORT FLIP*

colourfully sweetish. M.L.

2 cream
1 egg
1 tsp sugar
2 port

Shake briskly with ice. Strain into goblet. Sprinkle powdered nutmeg on top.

RUM MILK PUNCH*

invigoratingly sweet. L.

4 milk
1 tsp sugar
2 dark rum

Shake (or blend) briskly with crushed ice. Pour entire into tall glass. Sprinkle powdered nutmeg on top. Serve with straws.

RUM MOKA

richly sweet. L.

2 tblsp vanilla ice cream (or chocolate)
2 dark rum
1 tsp sugar
4 strong black coffee

Shake briskly (or blend) with crushed ice. Pour entire into tall glass. Optional: grate a little plain chocolate on top. Serve with straws.

SCOTCH SOLACE

differently and delicately sweet. L.

2 cream
4 milk
2 Scotch
1 tsp clear honey
1 tsp Cointreau

Shake (or blend) with ice. Strain into tall glass. Optional: grate a little orange peel on top.

SMITH & WESSON

semi-sweet. M.L.

2 cream
2 milk
1 ½ Tia Maria
Shake briskly with ice. Strain on-the-rocks into goblet. Top with a little soda-water.

SUNRISE   C

intriguingly sweet. M.L.

1 cream
1 tequila
½ Galliano
½ banana cream (optional)
1 tsp grenadine syrup
1 tsp lemon juice

Shake briskly with ice. Strain into large cocktail-glass.

(Banana-cream – crème de banane – can be made by mashing fully ripe banana with a little milk and sugar.)

S end your own cocktail recipes to us at Peter Dominic's Wine Mine Club, Vintner House, River Way, Harlow, Essex. (See page 152).

Pink Lady

VELVET GLOVES*

one of our specials: semi-sweet. S.

1 cream
1 Malibu
1 vodka
½ tsp sugar

Shake briskly with ice. Strain into cocktail-glass.

WHITE ELEPHANT*

new: medium-sweet. S.

1 cream
1 Bailey's Irish Cream
1 vodka

Shake briskly with ice. Strain into cocktail-glass. Decorate with cherry on stick.

WHITE MINK

a touch of sophistication: fairly sweet. M.L.

2 cream
1 Galliano
1 Tia Maria
½ brandy
2 tblsp vanilla ice cream

Shake briskly (or blend) with ice. Strain into goblet.

M ixes containing cream or related products are best made in shaker (or electric blender): a mixing glass may not give full combination of all ingredients.

SUNDRY SPIRIT COCKTAILS

There are various Cocktails – and other mixed drinks – which do not immediately fit into a particular spirit category.

ABSINTHE SPECIAL

strongly aniseedy: sweetish. S.

1 Pernod (or Ricard)
½ anisette
1 water
¼ tsp sugar

Shake with ice. Strain into cocktail-glass.

APPLE

powerfully medium-dry. S.

1 calvados
1½ sweet cider
½ gin
½ brandy

Stir with ice. Strain into cocktail-glass.

APPLEJACK RABBIT   C

on the dry side. M.L.

2 calvados
1 orange juice
2 tsp lemon juice
1 tsp sugar

Shake with ice. Strain into cocktail-glass.

BENTLEY

medium-dry. S.

1½ Dubonnet
1½ calvados

Shake with ice. Strain into cocktail-glass.

BULLDOG HIGHBALL

bracingly medium-sweet. L.

3 orange juice
1½ gin

Pour on-the-rocks in tall glass. Top with ginger ale.

CHICAGO

excitingly dry. L.

½ Cointreau
½ brandy
2 dashes Angostura

Pour over ice in tall glass or goblet with sugar-frosted rim. Top with chilled dry sparkling wine.

CO-OP*

ours: exhilaratingly sweetish. L.

1 Cointreau
1 Malibu
1 gin
1 tsp lemon juice

Shake with ice. Strain on-the-rocks into tall glass. Top with fizzy lemonade. Add slice of orange. Serve with straws.

EGG NOGG   C

M.L./L.

This is a mix of whole egg with any spirit – usually brandy, whisky or dark rum – or combination of spirits and wine. Milk and sweeteners are normal ingredients. Egg Noggs are of considerable antiquity: they were originally for invalids. They have retained social popularity in the U.S.A. in particular.

A typical cold Nogg is Baltimore (see Cream Cocktails). We give another recipe under Hot Drinks (Nogg).

Noggs are an area where the do-it-yourself initiative may find full scope.

GIN & GINGER* C

worthy revival. L.

Ginger beer does not have the great popularity it used to enjoy: it seems to have lost out to sweeter ginger ale. But gin and ginger beer is a splendid summer drink. Today's ginger beer benefits from sharpening – so an addition of lemon juice is recommended. It is also better if the ginger beer be well chilled rather than diluted by the drink being served on-the-rocks.

G & T*   C

suggestions on a tradition. L.

One might think the universal gin-and-tonic scarcely required mention here anymore than a whisky-and-soda. However, we would suggest trying it with a squeeze of lemon juice as well as the usual slice of lemon floating in

---

Quantities are expressed in number(s) or fractions of a measure of 1 fl. oz/25 ml capacity, except where other quantities are stated.

it. The author has even concocted a Super G & T:

1½ gin
½ Cointreau
1 lemon juice
½ orange juice

Pour on-the-rocks in tall glass. Top with tonic-water.

(Perhaps we should have included that recipe in the next chapter.)

GRIGIO VERDE

unusual: medium-sweet. S.

1½ grappa
1 crème de menthe

Stir with ice. Strain into cocktail-glass.

KISS ME QUICK

if your partner likes aniseed, sweetie. S.

1 Pernod (or Ricard)
½ Cointreau
3 dashes Angostura

Shake until very cold. Strain into cocktail-glass.

KITTY LOVE

medium-dry. S.

1 Cointreau
1 kirsch
1 dry vermouth (Carpano Punt è
  Mes preferably)
1 tsp orange juice

Shake with ice. Strain into cocktail-glass.

PLAYBOY

sleek and sweet. S.

½ apricot brandy
½ brandy
½ Cointreau
1 orange juice
2 tsps egg white

Shake with ice. Strain into sugar-frosted cocktail-glass.

ROUND THE WORLD

medium-sweet. M.L.

2 crème de menthe
3 pineapple juice
1 gin (or vodka)

Shake with ice. Strain into goblet. Garnish with pineapple cubes on stick.

SAVOY SPRINGBOK

distinctively medium-sweet. S.

1 Van der Hum
½ Lillet
½ dry sherry

Stir with ice. Strain into cocktail-glass.

SCARLETT O'HARA

sweeter than her temper. M.L.

2 Southern Comfort
2 cranberry juice
2 orange juice
1 tsp lemon juice

Shake with ice. Strain into goblet.

(Blackcurrant syrup might be substituted for cranberry.)

◀ **Gin and Tonic**

SLOE GLOW*

bitter-sweet. S.

2 sloe gin
1 red vermouth
½ lemon juice

Shake with ice. Strain into cocktail-glass.

SNOWBALL*   C

sweet. L.

2 advocaat
½ lemon juice

Pour over ice cubes in tall glass. Top with fizzy lemonade. Add slice of lemon.

SPRING BLOSSOM

medium-dry. S.

2 cherry brandy
1 brandy
½ tsp lemon juice
½ tsp grenadine syrup (or sugar)

Shake with ice. Strain into cocktail-glass.

STARBOARD LIGHT

medium-sweet. M.L.

1 sloe gin
½ crème de menthe
½ lemon juice

Shake with ice. Strain on to crushed ice in large cocktail-glass. Serve with straws.

SWEET & SOUR

self-descriptive. S.

1 Amer Picon
2 red vermouth
dash Angostura

Stir with ice. Strain into cocktail-glass.

VIKING

medium sweet. S.

1 aquavit
1 maraschino
1 lime juice cordial
1 tsp lemon juice

Shake with ice. Strain into cocktail-glass.

WHAT'S IT?

our recipe: your guess. L.

1½ Van der Hum
1 brandy
½ ginger wine
1 tsp lemon juice

Pour on-the-rocks in tall glass. Top with ginger ale. Decorate with round of orange. Serve with straws.

PARTY DRINKS & PUNCHES

For party entertainment, one can make up, in advance of their use, quantities of what are normally individual drinks that are prepared from one to four servings. For example, you can prepare a big jug of Bronx or Screwdriver cocktails – several others are suitable for this treatment – and keep under refrigeration until needed. A good instance of an admirable party drink that may be made in a big batch is the Bloody Mary. Simply multiply the amounts of ingredients.

Then there are drinks specifically designed for making in bulk. The following recipes are meant as guidelines. Some personal ingenuity may improve a mix, or get round the problem of absence of a particular ingredient. The strength of, say, a punch lies largely with you – and so does its degree of sweetness. It is desirable to taste a small trial quantity before committing yourself to producing a litre or so.

When you only have a few people to cater for, it is fun to run up some different cocktails. But if you are having a larger party, unless you wish to spend all your time as an amateur bartender – and some hosts do want to – it is an excellent notion to have a single focal drink. You can prepare at your leisure (and keep under refrigeration) as much as you think you will require (it will seldom be enough!) – with little or nothing to add when serving – and feel free to socialise. Also, it is a fact that party guests often like to be relieved from having to make a choice. You should, however, remember that some of your friends may not care for mixed drinks – so have a few straight ones in reserve, even if out of sight. And do not forget non-drinkers of alcohol: we have not, as a later section shows.

The number of servings per recipe are broad estimates: we cannot know how generous are your glasses.

BACCIO PUNCH C

(14 servings)

1 standard bottle gin
1½ pints (850 ml) grapefruit juice
     (sweetened)
4 fl. oz (10 ml) Pernod

Mix in large bowl/jug with plenty of ice. Add any fresh or canned fruit according to availability. Just before serving, add bottle of chilled sparkling wine. Serve in stemmed glasses with some fruit.

BOURBON FOG C

(10 servings)

1 pint (½ litre) vanilla ice cream
1 pint (½ litre) very strong black
     coffee (cold)
½ standard bottle Bourbon (or
     other whisky)

Mix thoroughly and refrigerate, without freezing. No added ice. Serve in goblets with a dusting of powdered cinnamon.

CIDER CUP

(30 servings)

2 pints (1 litre) medium-
sweet still cider
10 fl. oz (300 ml) vodka
1 pint (½ litre) orange juice
5 fl. oz (150 ml) lemon juice
5 fl. oz (150 ml) Cointreau
     (optional); or 3 oz (75 g)
     sugar.

Chill the cider. Mix all ingredients in large bowl(s)/jug(s), with rounds of orange and other fruit to hand. Add ice cubes and stir. Add siphon soda-water just before serving. Serve in stemmed glasses, with an ice cube in each.

CLARET CUP

(10 servings)

1 standard bottle red wine
1 sliced orange
1 sliced lemon
8 rounds of pineapple (canned),
     not cubes.
2 fl. oz (50 ml) Cointreau
2 fl. oz (50 ml) brandy
2 fl. oz (50 ml) lemon juice
1 tblsp sugar

Put the fruit into big bowl/jug. Add other ingredients and plenty of ice cubes – or refrigerate fully. Just before serving, add siphon soda-water. Serve in stemmed glasses with pieces of fruit.

JOHN'S BOWL *

(14 servings)

1 standard bottle vodka or gin
5 fl. oz (125 ml) Cointreau
3 fl. oz (75 ml) brandy
5 fl. oz (125 ml) lemon juice
2 tblsp sugar

Mix well in suitable bowl/jug with plenty of ice. Add rounds of cucumber and orange. Just before serving, add large bottle of fizzy lemonade. Serve in goblets with rounds of lemon.

RED WINE PUNCH

(24 servings)

2 pints (l litre) strong red wine
1 standard bottle Ruby port (or
     port wine style)
½ bottle cherry brandy
4 oz (100 g) brown sugar
5 fl. oz (125 ml) orange juice
3 fl. oz (100 ml) lemon juice

Mix with ice in large bowl(s)/jug(s). Just before serving, add siphon soda-water. Serve in stemmed glasses decorated with cherry on stick.

SHERRY PUNCH

(16 servings)

1 bottle medium-dry sherry
½ bottle brandy
2 tblsp each of Cointreau
    maraschino
    grenadine syrup
1 siphon soda-water

Mix in large bowl(s)/jug(s), adding fruit as available. Refrigerate thoroughly. Just before serving, add 1 bottle chilled sparkling wine (the sweeter, inexpensive Italian Moscato is quite suitable here).

SPARKLING PUNCH

(16 servings)

2 bottles good quality dry sparkling
    wine
5 fl. oz (125 ml) brandy
3 fl. oz (75 ml) Cointreau
3 fl. oz (75 ml) maraschino (or
    grenadine syrup)

Mix ingredients, without undue stirring, as late as possible before required, with some ice. Refrigerate until serving time. Serve in stemmed glasses, without added ice.

WASHINGTON COOLER

(20 servings)

1 bottle robust red wine
½ bottle dark rum
1 pint (575 ml) orange juice
4 oz (100 g) sugar

Mix in bowl(s)/jug(s) and refrigerate. Just before serving, add siphon soda-water. Serve in stemmed glasses with 2 ice cubes and half-round of orange.

◄ **Sparkling punch**

NOT ORIGINALLY FOR JUDY

PUNCH gained its name from India. Early British forebears of the Raj found solace in long cold mixes containing local produce: Arrack, distilled by the Dutch in what is now Indonesia, was the nearest commercial spirit. For no apparent reason, it became a custom to use five ingredients – spirits, tea (from China in those days), sugar, fruit juice and water were basics. The Hindi for five is *pantsch* – quickly translated, with the typical British disdain for alien tongues, into Punch.

Punches, cold or hot, are admirable for serving to fairly large numbers of people. They were extremely popular for at least two centuries, going into a decline after the first World War, but recently returning to favour. Again we see on sale modern punch-bowls with matching glasses. Today these – and they are not always expensive – are usually in glass, but silver-plated ones are also made, and even sterling replicas of the antique ones that are themselves extremely costly. Antique punch ladles need not be an extravagance: they have survived in large numbers.

WHITE WINE PUNCH

(18 servings)

2 pints (1 litre) medium-dry white
    wine
½ bottle dry sherry
5 fl. oz (125 ml) brandy
4 fl. oz (100 ml) lemon juice
½ pint (275 ml) strong cold tea

Mix in large bowl(s)/jug(s) and refrigerate. Just before serving, add siphon soda-water. Garnish with rounds of cucumber. Serve in goblets with 2 ice cubes and round of cucumber.

HOT PUNCHES

ALE FLIP

(12 servings)

2 pints (1 litre) strong dark beer
5 eggs
5 oz (150 g) brown sugar
5 fl. oz (150 ml) brandy
2 lemons

Finely grate peel from lemons and add to the beer in suitable saucepan. Heat gradually, without boiling, and then mix in other ingredients slowly and thoroughly, keeping mixture hot. Ladle into warmed glass or china mugs and sprinkle powdered nutmeg on top.

(Modern saucepans are decorative enough to bring into the room where there are guests to be served. Glass ones are highly suitable: copper ones are pretty and also conserve heat well. Any form of plate-warmer, at low heat, will keep the drink at good temperature.)

RED WINE MULL

(30 servings)

2 pints (1 litre) robust red table wine
½ bottle Ruby port (or port style wine)
5 fl. oz (150 ml) brandy
2 tsp powdered cinnamon
1 tsp powdered red nutmeg
2 oz (50 g) brown sugar
1 lemon
8 cloves

Stick the cloves into the lemon and put with other ingredients in suitable saucepan(s). Heat slowly, stirring often, until as hot as possible without boiling. Taste: add more sugar if not sweet enough. Ladle into warmed mugs.

TEA PUNCH

(20 servings)

½ bottle dark rum
½ bottle brandy
½ lb (225 g) brown sugar
2 pints (1 litre) strained strong tea
2 tblsp lemon juice

Heat slowly, without boiling, and stir frequently, in suitable saucepan. Ladle into warmed glass or china mugs with a pinch of powdered cinnamon.

A couple of considerably more elaborate punches will be found in the following chapter (8).

HOT DRINKS

Following the final recipes in the previous section, it is logical to append a few individual hot alcoholic mixes. Hot drinks of this sort are not very widely popular in Britain today; the preferred hot potions are mainly of the proprietary non-alcoholic variety. Yet, not so long ago our forebears revelled in hot spicy concoctions, particularly Noggs and the Negus. The following all have tradition behind them.

BLACK STRIPE

2 dark rum
1 tblsp honey

Mix in warmed china mug or strong glass. Top with boiling water. Stir.

BRANDY TOT

1½ brandy
¼ tsp allspice
2 tsp sugar

Put into warmed stemmed glass or mug. Add slice of orange peel. Top with mixture of boiling milk and water. Stir.

CARIBBEAN SWIZZLE

2 dark rum
1 tsp brown sugar
1 tsp lemon juice

Put into warmed glass or china mug. Top with boiling water. Stir.

GLÜHWEIN

2 tsp brown sugar
½ tsp powdered cinnamon
slice of lemon

Place in warmed glass and pour in about 10 fl. oz (275 ml) of hot red table wine.

(This is one form of the much favoured German winter warmer.)

Left to right: Nogg, Port Negus
and Whisky Toddy (all recipes
on page 128)

THE ADMIRAL'S LEGACY

GROG has rather a different meaning now, when used at all, to its original one. It was coined as a derogatory slang phrase to describe dilution with water for Ordinary Seamen of the Royal Navy's rum ration. This was ordered by Admiral Vernon in the 18th century.

The Admiral's nickname was Old Grog, from the grogram (coarse silk) cloak he habitually wore, and the transference of Grog from person to thing was quite logical.

Later Grog was applied to any spirits with water. Today its application is mainly as given in our recipe.

PORT NEGUS

2 Ruby port
1 tsp sugar

Dissolve sugar in port in warmed stemmed glass. Add hot water. Stir. Dust with powdered nutmeg. See illustration on page 127.

TAM O'SHANTER

2 Scotch
1 dark rum
1 tsp brown sugar

Mix in warmed glass. Top with boiling water. Sprinkle on top a little allspice.

WHISKY TODDY

Dissolve 2 tsp sugar in a little hot water in warmed tumbler. Add 2 Scotch. Stir. Top with boiling water and add a little more Scotch, without stirring.

(Traditionally, any Scotch toddy is stirred with a sterling silver spoon – presumably with an Edinburgh hallmark. See illustration on page 127.)

GROG

2 dark rum
2 tsp lemon juice
1 tsp brown sugar
¼ tsp powdered cinnamon
4 sultanas

Put ingredients in warmed mug. Top with boiling water. Stir.

(Grog is a term covering various spirituous drinks.)

NOGG

1 tsp sugar
1 brandy
1 dark rum
1 egg

Beat thoroughly in warmed mug. Top with boiling milk. Sprinkle with powdered nutmeg.

(Noggs, always containing egg, may be hot or cold. They may be made with any preferred spirit, brandy, whisky and rum being the most suitable. See illustration on page 127.)

Quantities are expressed in number(s) or fractions of a measure of 1 fl. oz/25 ml capacity, except where other quantities are stated.

NON–SPIRIT COCKTAILS

There are a number of interesting – sometimes Classic – mixes which, though mildly alcoholic, do not contain elements customarily known as spirits. We separate them (which is not usually done) for the benefit of people who prefer this style of drink.

ADONIS*

medium-dry. S.

2 dry sherry
1 red vermouth
dash Angostura

Stir briefly with ice. Strain into cocktail-glass.

AMERICANO   C

cryptically bitter-sweet. M.L.

1 red vermouth
½ Campari

Pour on-the-rocks in goblet. Top with soda-water. Stir briefly. Add half-round of orange.

BAMBOO*

medium-dry. S.

1 dry sherry
1 red vermouth
½ dry vermouth

Stir with ice. Strain into cocktail-glass.

Send your own cocktail recipes to us at Peter Dominic's Wine Mine Club, Vintner House, River Way, Harlow, Essex. (See page 152).

BISHOP   C

medium-dry. L.

1 tblsp sugar
½ tsp lemon juice
1 tblsp orange juice

Dissolve above in tall glass. Add several ice cubes. Top with light red wine. Stir. Decorate with available fruit. Serve with straws.

(This is an American style of Bishop. Another, very different mix of the same name will be found in Chapter 8.)

CIDER COOLER*

enlivening: semi-sweet. L.

5 dry cider
3 orange juice
1 lemon juice
2 grenadine syrup (or 1 tblsp sugar)

Pour over ice cubes in tall glass. Serve with straws.

CLARET REFRESHER*

vinously medium-dry. L.

4 red wine
2 orange juice
1 lemon juice
2 tsp sugar

Shake briskly with ice. Strain into tall glass. Add squirt of soda-water. Decorate with round of orange.

DEVIL'S OWN

he's welcome: bitter-sweet. S.

2 port
1 dry vermouth
½ tsp lemon juice

Shake with ice. Strain into cocktail-glass.

DIABOLO

sweetish. S.

2 Dubonnet
½ lemon
1 tsp grenadine syrup

Shake with ice. Strain into cocktail-glass. Add cherry on stick.

JEREZ

dry. S.

2 dry sherry
dash Angostura
1 tsp orange juice

Stir with ice. Strain into cocktail-glass.

KLONDYKE*

medium-dry. M.L.

1 red vermouth
1 dry vermouth
2 lemon juice
1 tsp sugar

Shake with ice. Strain into goblet with 2 ice cubes. Top with American ginger ale.

OPORTO

rather richly sweetish. L.

3 port
2 lemon juice
2 tsp sugar
1 tsp grenadine

Shake ingredients with ice. Strain into tall glass optionally with frosted rim. Top with dry sparkling wine.

PORT FLIP*

medium-sweet. M.L.

3 port
1 tsp sugar
1 egg yolk

Shake briskly with ice. Strain into large cocktail-glass. Dust top with powdered cinnamon.

(Also made with medium-dry sherry.)

SHERRY COBBLER

semi-sweet. L.

3 dry sherry
1 tsp sugar
1 tsp grenadine syrup

Mix with a little soda-water in tall glass. Add ice. Top with soda-water. Stir briefly. Decorate with fruit in season.

VERMOUTH CASSIS*

bitter-sweet. M.L.

2 dry vermouth
1 crème de cassis (or blackcurrant syrup)

Stir on-the-rocks in small glass. Optional: add a little soda-water.

WHITE WINE ZIP

revivingly sweetish. L.

5 medium-dry white table wine
2 lemon juice

Shake or stir briefly. Strain into tall glass with 2 ice cubes. Top with quality orange squash. Serve with straws.

NON-ALCOHOLIC DRINKS

Some twenty years ago, the author coined the word 'Mocktail' to describe an interesting, but totally non-intoxicant, mix. The term Cocktail has an essentially alcoholic connotation. To talk of a 'non-alcoholic cocktail' has the same linguistic contradiction as a 'nut cutlet'. Mocktail has, flatteringly, gone into the vocabulary of drinking: it no longer has the novelty of a gimmick name. The simpler heading to this section is descriptive enough.

Non-alcoholic drinks have interest beyond the needs of abstainers. There are times when we all relish an attractive, long, cool drink without any alcoholic content – or even a short substitute for our usual more stimulating aperitif. It is pleasing to offer guests who do not take alcohol – or who cherish their driving licences – something more exciting than an orange squash or bottled soft drink. And we may – momentarily in the context of this book – think of children. Why should they not have a festive drink that looks like an adult cocktail?

ACAPULCO

4 pineapple juice
2 grapefruit juice
2 cream
1 tsp sugar

Shake with crushed ice. Pour entire into tall glass. Decorate with pineapple cubes on stick. Serve with straws.

BLOODY VIRGIN

This is the famous Bloody Mary (see Vodka cocktails) undefiled by spirit!

CINDERELLA

2 pineapple juice
2 lemon juice
2 orange juice

Shake with ice. Strain on-the-rocks into tall glass. Top with soda-water. Decorate with cherries on stick. Serve with straws. Optional: float ½ tsp grenadine syrup on top.

CAPUCINE

1 peppermint cordial
3 cream
1 oz (25 g) grated plain chocolate

Shake briskly with ice. Strain into large cocktail-glass.

(Though we have carefully not recommended it elsewhere, it is just possible to use peppermint cordial in some cocktails in place of Crème de Menthe.)

FIRST AID

2 lemon juice
2 tsp blackcurrant syrup
½ tsp sugar

Mix in tumbler with crushed ice. Add slice of lemon. Top with soda-water. Serve with straw.

LIMEY

2 Rose's lime juice cordial
1 lemon juice
1 tsp egg white

Shake briskly with ice. Strain into cocktail-glass.

LONG BOAT

2 Rose's lime juice cordial
1 tsp lemon juice

Pour over ice cubes in tall glass. Top with ginger beer. Decorate with mint sprig when available.

MINTY

Crush 2 minted sprigs in tumbler with 2 grenadine syrup (or 1 tblsp sugar).

Add 2 ice cubes. Top with chilled ginger ale. Decorate with round of lemon.

Quantities are expressed in number(s) or fractions of a measure of 1 fl. oz/25 ml capacity, except where other quantities are stated.

PARSON'S PARTICULAR

2 orange juice
1 lemon juice
½ tsp grenadine syrup
yolk of 1 egg

Shake briskly with ice. Strain into large cocktail-glass.

PROHIBITION

3 blackcurrant syrup poured over 2 ice cubes in tall glass.

Add any fruit to hand. Top with chilled fizzy-lemondade.

PUSSYFOOT   C

1 orange juice
1 lemon juice
1 lime juice cordial
yolk of 1 egg

Shake briskly with ice. Strain into large cocktail-glass. Add splash soda-water. See illustration on page 132.

SLIM JIM   C

3 tomato juice
3 grapefruit juice
¼ tsp Worcester sauce

Shake with ice. Strain into large cocktail-glass. Add slice of lemon.

(Or use orange instead of grapefruit juice, in which case the drink becomes a Slim Jane.)

SPORTSMAN

1 lime juice cordial
1 lemon juice
½ tsp rose-hip syrup (or grenadine)

Pour over ice cubes in tall glass. Top with tonic-water.

TEMPERANCE TANKARD

Into ½-pint glass tankard put a few slices of cucumber, apple and orange.
Add 2 orange juice
Top with well-chilled apple juice

If extra ice added, only a little.

TONGA

2 pineapple juice
2 lemon juice
white of 1 egg
1 tsp grenadine syrup

Shake with ice. Strain into tall glass with 2 ice cubes. Top with chilled fizzy lemonade. Add fruit at discretion. Serve with straws.

T.T.

4 grape juice (red or white)
1 lemon juice

Stir with ice. Strain into large cocktail-glass. Decorate with cherry on stick.

YELLOW LION

1 tblsp cream
2 tsp golden syrup
1 tsp lemon juice

Shake well with ice. Strain into large cocktail-glass. Add squirt of soda-water.

Obviously, the above recipes are capable of infinite personal variation. Though a few are quite established, this is a field wide open to ingenuity in matters of colour and taste. On question of colour, remember that ice cubes may easily be coloured by using a few drops of flavourless food-colouring in freezer-tray. This can add visual allure to slightly boring drinks. Also, most drinks here lend themselves to having the rims of their serving glasses frosted. One may also colour the frosting by drops of colouring mixed with moistened caster sugar. (Frosting is explained in Chapter 6.)

Of course, there is nothing to stop you jazzing up any of these drinks with vodka or gin – but please do *not* try any tricks on abstainers: there are few worse social misdemeanours.

◀ **Pussyfoot**

RESTORATIVE COCKTAILS

It is not necessarily to suggest that our readers suffer ever from that consequence of over-indulgence vulgarly known as a 'hangover' that we include this short section. There are times, however, when the most moderate of us feel less than entirely well in the morning: the cause is immaterial. We need bucking up.

It is sometimes pointed out that the 'hair of the dog' theory is fallacious. It is vaguely based on a homoeopathic notion. But if the unpleasing condition happens to be due to injudious intake of alcohol, is it likely to be corrected by further swallowing of the same beverages? Simple sweet fruit drinks, or only just water, are prescribed in some quarters.

Yet the magic – real or imagined – of certain strong potions (Cocktails many of them) remains powerfully entrenched in many minds. And, after all, if you think something is benefitting you, then it probably is.

The restorative virtues of some mixes elsewhere dealt with in a more sociable climate are a matter for personal opinion. Highly thought of as morning-after drinks are Bloody Mary, Bullshot, and Buck's Fizz. Underberg and Fernet Branca are proprietary bitters with strong therapeutic claims. Black Velvet (Chapter 9) is popular.

Certain specific recipes have over the years gained a widespread reputation as harbingers of at least temporary relief from self-induced internal disorders.

PICK-ME-UP*

2 brandy
1 tsp sugar
dash Angostura
½ pint (275 ml) milk

Shake well with ice. Strain into tall glass. Squirt of soda-water. Drink slowly.

SAVOY CORPSE-REVIVER   C

1 brandy
1 crème de menthe
1 Fernet Branca

Shake fully with ice. Strain into cocktail-glass.

YANKEE INVIGORATOR   C

1 brandy
2 port
1 egg
½ pint (275 ml) strong black coffee
2 tsp brown sugar

Shake vigorously with ice. Strain into tall glass.

(Perhaps this is rather too pleasant to do much good!)

CORPSE REVIVER*

1 brandy
½ red vermouth
½ lemon juice

Stir with ice. Strain into cocktail-glass.

HEART STARTER

2 gin in about 5 fl. oz iced water in tumbler.
Add 2 tsp liver salts

Toss quickly 'down the hatch'.

DOG'S HAIR

1 Scotch
2 cream
1 tsp honey
½ tsp lemon juice
dash Angostura

Shake with ice. Strain into large cocktail-glass one-third filled with crushed ice. Serve with straw.

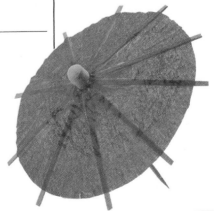

DON'T BURY ME ON THE LONE PRAIRIE!

Folk lore has it that when a band of pioneers were exploring the vast prairies of the U.S.A., one of their number fell grievously ill. In his delirium he called desperately for oysters. There was, of course, none for thousands of miles. But one of his companions had an idea. He found some wild turkey's eggs. Putting a couple of these in a mug, he added pepper and salt and fortified it with whiskey. He thought this might prove a restorative, or at least ease the sick man's final hours. Taking the mug, the demented invalid saw the egg. 'Ah, oysters!' he cried with joy, and downed the lot. 'Let me have more oysters'. Almost miraculously, his energy returned and shortly he was well enough to continue the journey.

Well, you don't have to believe that was the original PRAIRIE OYSTER, yet it's a pretty tale.

PRAIRIE OYSTER   C

Slide into large cocktail-glass
1 large egg yolk (intact)
Put on top ½ brandy
1 tsp Worcester sauce
½ tsp wine vinegar
dash of salt
½ tsp tomato ketchup
Sprinkle a touch of cayenne
    pepper

Pour into mouth in one go and let it trickle down to stimulate a sluggish stomach.

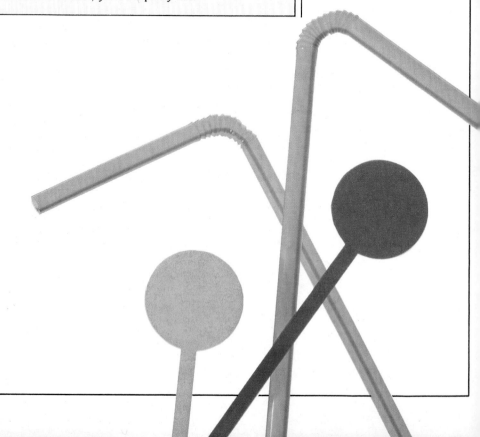

Advanced Course

Uniquely, we believe, amongst cocktail guides, we have hitherto listed no recipes that are not within the competence and resources of anyone at all interested in the subject. We have maintained a declared intention of being highly practical, have avoided extravagant recipes or those calling for ingredients not easily found.

Yet we feel we should devote a little space to the encouragement of those who have acquired an inclination towards more exotic, even curious, compounds. There is a vast repertoire. In the author's personal library at least 6000 recipes are recorded – of which he deems only about 500 are worth serious consideration. Of these he invented several (he is too modest to indicate which).

So we can do no more than make a representative selection. We continue to avoid, whilst becoming marginally more elaborate, any of the truly esoteric – often ridiculous – compounds of the past, or of the present for that matter. We deem it best to allow sensible combinations to inspire our readers. Cocktails should amuse and stimulate, not astound the palate.

ADAM & EVE

chic: semi-sweet. S.

1 Forbidden Fruit liqueur
1 gin
1 brandy
¼ tsp lemon juice.

Shake with ice. Strain into cocktail-glass.

BLIMLET

provokingly bitter-sweet. M.L.

2 gin
1 Rose's lime juice cordial
½ lime juice (freshly squeezed)
½ crème de cassis

Stir with ice. Strain on-the-rocks into sugar-frosted large cocktail-glass. Top with chilled Perrier water.

Quantities are expressed in number(s) or fractions of a measure of 1 fl. oz/25 ml capacity, except where other quantities are stated.

BISHOP or ENGLISH BISHOP C

(18 servings) aromatically enlivening.

Into 2 washed oranges stick a dozen cloves each

Bake slowly in moderate oven until lightly browned

Cut prepared oranges into quarters and place in suitable saucepan

Pour in 2 bottles Ruby port

Heat slowly, taking care not to boil

Add 3 oz (75 ml) brown sugar

4 brandy

2 dark rum

2 tsp powdered cinnamon

Allow to remain heating (not boiling), covered, for about an hour

Serve in decorative mugs with sprinkle of powdered nutmeg on top.

(Amount of spirits, and spices, may be adjusted to individual taste. Test for sweetness during preparation.)

CAFE ROYAL

sweetly warming. M.L.

2 yellow Chartreuse

1 lump of sugar

Place in large coffee-cup. Pour on top superior real black coffee (strong). Stir.

CARIBBEAN DAWN

(for 2 servings) enticingly, delicately sweetish. M.L.

3 Malibu

2 tequila

3 tblsp strawberry ice cream

½ tsp strawberry syrup (*fraise*)

Put into blender with 3 tblsp crushed ice. Blend no more than 15 seconds. Pour (without straining) into two goblets. Decorate with fresh strawberries. Serve with decorative straws.

Caribbean Dawn

Send your own cocktail recipes to us at Peter Dominic's Wine Mine Club, Vintner House, River Way, Harlow, Essex. (See page 152).

CASINO DE PARIS

*beautifully bracing: medium-dry.
M.L.*

2 brandy
1 apricot brandy
½ maraschino
½ lemon juice

*Shake with ice. Strain into large
goblet. Top with Champagne (well
chilled). No added ice. Decorate
with round of orange.*

CHAMPAGNE COCKTAIL   C

*classy, exciting, and extravagant.
M.L.*

In a goblet or large flute glass (not
    a saucer-glass) place:
1 lump of sugar
2 dashes of Angostura on the
    sugar

*Top with very cold dry
Champagne (good quality)*

(There are many variations on this
Classic theme.)

EROTICA

bitter-sweet labour of love. L.

Into a large goblet put:
slices of fresh peach, strawberries
    and grapes (de-pipped)
Stir in 1 heaped tablespoon of
    crushed ice
Add 2 tsp grenadine
1 tsp each Cointreau, maraschino,
    cherry brandy, kirsch, brandy
Stir
Top with very cold dry
    Champagne.

*Decorate with cocktail cherries on
stick. Serve with decorative straws
(with silver spoon handy).*
See illustration on page 138.

Champagne Cocktail ▶

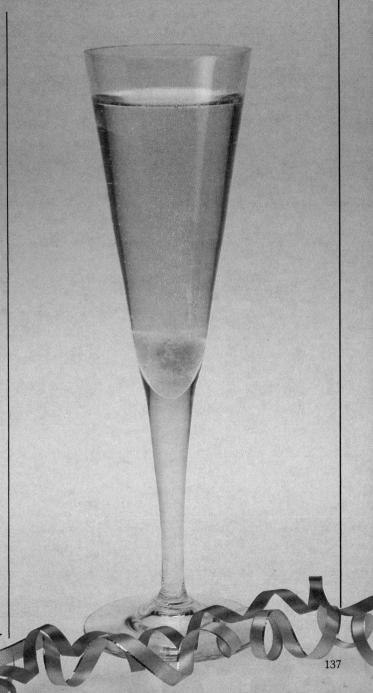

FISH HOUSE PUNCH   C

(30 servings) enigmatically stimulating.

Blend carefully:
2 bottles dark rum
1 bottle brandy
14 oz (400 g) brown sugar
3 pints (1½ litres) water
3 tsp peach bitters
2 tsp orange bitters

Pour blended ingredients into large punch-bowl containing big lumps of ice. Stir, and serve, as soon as cold, in stemmed glasses.

(This is an 18th century American drink, probably from Philadelphia, of which there are numerous versions)

KNOCKOUT

and a winner on points: dry. L.

1½ brandy
2 tsp grenadine
1 tsp sugar
yolk of 1 egg

Shake briskly with ice. Strain into tall glass. Top with chilled dry Champagne.

LICHEE

a sweetish glance Eastwards. M.L.

1 gin
1 dry vermouth
2 lichee syrup
2 dashes Angostura

Shake with ice. Strain into large cocktail-glass. Decorate with (fresh peeled) lichee on stick.

◀ **Erotica (recipe on page 137)**

LOUISIANA

an amusing variation. M.L.

2 vodka
3 tomato juice
1 tsp lemon juice
dashes of Tabasco, Worcester
    sauce, red pepper

Pour on to 'olive ice cubes' in goblet. Add splash of soda-water. Note: To produce 'olive ice cubes' – Put pimento-stuffed green olives in units in freezer-tray. Top with water and freeze normally.

PIMMS ROYALE

mutations of an old friend. L.

Pimms (Chapter 9) made with
    chilled dry Champagne: only
    add slice of orange.

PIMMS SPECIAL

Pimms made normally but with
    additional zest of
2 gin or vodka
1 Cointreau

(Neither of these versions is much favoured by the proprietors.)

PLANTER'S PUNCH   C

bitter-sweet inspiration from W. Indies. L.

We have given a simplified edition under Rum Cocktails. There is no established recipe. Traditionally, it is proportionally composed of one Sour (lime), two Sweet (sugar), three Strong (rum), and four Weak (water/ice). Here is the recipe from a Planter's Punch specialist in the British Virgin Islands. His preference is for golden Barbados or Trinidad rum and sugar syrup made by boiling local raw brown sugar, and he does not follow traditional order:
1 sugar syrup
3 fresh lime juice
3 rum
1 dash of grenadine

Shake vigorously with about 5 ice cubes. Pour entire into tall glass, pre-chilled. Garnish only with large twist of lime peel. Sprinkle with powdered nutmeg.

SINGAPORE GIN SLING   C

shades of Empire: bitter-sweet. L.

2 gin
½ lemon juice
½ Cointreau
½ cherry brandy
2 tsp sugar

Pour over ice cubes in tall glass. Stir well. Top with soda-water. Decorate with slice of lemon. Serve with straws.

Quantities are expressed in number(s) or fractions of a measure of 1 fl. oz/25 ml capacity, except where other quantities are stated.

TOM & JERRY   C

hot. (about 6 servings)
aromatically delicious. M.L.

Beat separately the yolks and
  whites of 12 eggs
Into the yolks beat ½ lb (225 g)
  sugar and 1 tblsp each of
  powdered cinnamon, allspice
  and cloves
Add 6 dark rum.
Stir. Fold in the beaten egg whites.

Put a tablespoon of this mixture in
a mug (for each serving) of about
½-pint capacity. Add 2 whisky
(whatever type you like). Top with
boiling hot mixture of milk and
water. Dust top of each drink with
powdered nutmeg.

(This is another celebrated
American punch.)

VERY IMPORTANT PERSONS

they have to be, for this. M.L.

2 gin
1 Pimms
2 passion fruit juice
½ dry vermouth
½ lemon juice

Shake briskly. Strain into goblet.
The original garnish was a white
water lotus nut on stick, but you
may have to settle for a
maraschino cherry.

ZOMBIE

supernaturally strong rarity. L.

1 pineapple juice (unsweetened)
1 papaya juice
2 lime juice
1 sugar
1 apricot brandy
3 dark rum

Shake with ice. Pour entire into
pre-chilled tall glass. If required,
add more ice almost to top.
Decorate with mint sprig in season,
and cube of pineapple and a
cherry on stick. Float of top 1 extra
strong dark rum. Sprinkle with
powdered nutmeg. Serve with
straws.

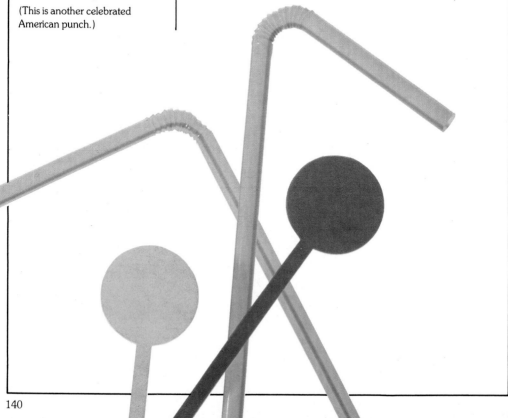

Miscellaneous Matters

We have said that it is hard to define a cocktail. We think that to include a few well-favoured drinks would be stretching the word:

For instance . . .

Pimms might by some be described as a cocktail since Pimm's No. 1 Cup is 'the Original Gin Sling' – and a sling is certainly a cocktail. However, Pimm's is unique, a proprietary mix. It was evolved in the 1840s by James Pimm for patrons of his oyster bar in the City of London, which flourished on a site where had stood a tavern mentioned as early as 1499. Pimm's successors decided to bottle his elixir. It was a great success, particularly with administrators in far-flung posts of the British Empire. It is a splendid summer party drink. Do follow the makers' instructions, and avoid the bar habit of dolling it up like a mildly alcoholic fruit salad.

Pink gin is not as popular as it used to be. It was associated with the officers of the Royal Navy and Plymouth gin, which used to be a specially aromatic type. It may be surmised that gin was originally added to medicinal anti-fever bitters, in the tropics, to make them easier to take. When Angostura bitters (Chapter 3) came on the scene, naval officers on the Caribbean station found it pleasing, adding a peculiar tang to gin and an attractive colour: Pink Gin became a social habit, not a health ritual. Pink gin is made by putting several dashes of Angostura into a tumbler or goblet, swilling them around briefly and then shaking out all but what cling to the surface. Add gin to your requirments and top with a little chilled water (ice optional) or soda-water.

Kir has in recent times been discovered by the British, though it still remains comparatively little drunk in the UK – a pity. It was originated by a famous French priest, Canon Kir, who also managed to become senior member of the National Assembly (the country's parliament) and was for years Mayor of Dijon. He died in 1968, aged 92, and the popularity of his tipple has increased in France ever since. In its true form it is a teaspoon of *crème de cassis* in the bottom of a wine-glass, on to which is poured chilled Bourgogne Aligoté (a crisp light white burgundy) or the stronger Chablis (very dry white Burgundy). You do need really dry white wine – it need not be Chablis. However, blackcurrant syrup (make sure it is proper syrup) will perform almost undetectably the magic of the *crème*. You don't have to tell your guests!

Irish coffee is said to have been evolved not by a bartender but by the head chef at Shannon Airport, Eire, just after World War II. The official instructions:

Warm a stemmed wine-glass. Put in a measure of Irish whiskey, sugar (to your taste), and very hot (strong) black coffee. Stir well. Over the back of a teaspoon carefully pour cream so it forms a layer up to ½ cm. thick. Do not stir: drink through the cream.

Atholl brose comes in two forms; we give the 'cocktail' one in Chapter 7. The more traditional form is very different: it is a mixture, to individual taste, of Scotch whisky, finely ground oatmeal, honey and, optionally, cream. This is left to stand for a few days. Unless this is well diluted with whisky or cream it is more food than drink – a sort of alcoholic porridge.

Black velvet is extraordinarily simple – and invigorating. In a tankard mix (half-and-half) Guinness and chilled non-vintage champagne. Ideally the Guinness should be draught, not bottled. It is not the same with other sparkling wines, but if the stout is a bit too tart for you, use a sweet (Moscato) Italian *spumante*, which has the merit of inexpensiveness at least.

Buck's fizz is another two-ingredient champagne mix – fifty-fifty fresh orange juice and chilled wine. This can be quite satisfactorily made with other dry sparkling wine of good quality.

Rusty nail is another mix one cannot really term a cocktail. It is a digestive blend, in

Rusty Nail

whatever proportions or quantities you wish, of Drambuie and Scotch whisky.

B & B is the Gallic version of the Rusty Nail – half-and-half Bénédictine and Cognac brandy.

Sloe gin is a cordial which it is well worth the trouble of making when sloes (the berries of the blackthorn) are in good supply. Wash and then individually prick sufficient sloes. Half-fill a standard (75 cl) clear bottle with these sloes. Add white granulated sugar to a depth of two inches on top of the fruit. Fill with gin. Close bottle and shake well, continuing to shake the bottle whenever you remember to during at least three months. Strain into other bottle(s): you get about ⅔ standard bottle of sloe gin per bottle of sloes, sugar and spirit. Vodka may be used. After making and straining, you can adjust sweetness by adding more sugar or lessen sweetness by adding spirit. Sloe gin is said to improve in bottle.

Sangria is, correctly, simply 2 teaspoons of sugar in a tall glass, dissolved with any preferred wine: add ice and top with more of same wine. It is now often garnished with fruit. Bottled Sangria is produced in Spain, and available (Garcia) in Britain.

Whisky mac is a mixture of Scotch and ginger wine in whatever proportions you care for. It is a winter warmer and should not – but can be – iced.

Mead is the honey-based brew of immense antiquity. Something like it was known in ancient Babylonian civilisation. Britons were drinking it when the Romans invaded. It was commonly used until

Henry VIII's dissolution of monasteries. It gradually became a comparative rarity: Charles II is recorded as drinking it occasionally instead of sweet wine. It is again made commercially in Sussex and Cornwall. If you happen to have some – perhaps bought on an excursion – you could use it in a mixed drink in place of honey (experimentally).

Pousse café is an oddity – possibly invented in New Orleans' red light district in the last century. It consists of layers of liqueurs (always an odd, 5–9, number) in a special, narrow glass called after the mix. Today, owing to changes in viscosity of liqueurs (their specific gravity if you want to be technical), it is not practicable to give a recipe that will work. It is not worth doing in any case.

Sake is with some accuracy referred to as 'rice wine'. It is a double fermentation of around 18% alcohol. It is now sold in Britain, though a long way to achieving the popularity of other Japanese products. It is drunk warmed in tiny tots and is certainly the right accompaniment to Japanese food, but has no cocktail applications; well, not in the West.

There are a few very varied topics related to social drinking, and making up drinks at home, which deserve mention but which do not fit logically into previous chapters: some are included just for instructive entertainment

Toast. We drink a toast to individuals, to organisations: the loyal toast to the Queen is proposed at thousands of functions every day. We often toast someone at home on special occasions. Do we ever consider what an odd expression it is, 'to drink a toast'? Surely, one would expect to eat it! The practice of drinking to health and good fortune is of enormous antiquity: to describe the action as a toast is probably no more than 350 years old. It does indeed derive from toasted, spiced bread, then frequently put into wine to add interest. 'Toast' then started being applied to the person whose health was being drunk: 'toast of the town', referring to some notable beauty, lingered long after toast had ceased to be put into wine. Toast is now noun and verb, and used with a drinking connotation in many countries in which it is linguistically alien.

Booze is a cosily rude sort of word. Some say it comes from an ancient falconry term describing a bird's action when drinking, but an old English derivation seems more likely: *bousen* – to drink deep.

Plonk is losing its derogatory meaning and becoming a piece of affectionate slang for sound, inexpensive wine of just the type for mixed drinks. It is almost certainly of World War I origin, 'plink plonk' being an Anglicisation of the French *vin blanc* – simple white wine of the sort soldiers drank in village cafés . The Australians are credited with putting 'plonk' into general circulation. Such are semantic changes that today you may hear someone say, as he pours a costly vintage, 'I think you'll find this quite a decent drop of plonk.'

Tea is part of some interesting punches. It is unlikely to be the brew you would give friends tea-time: it should be extra-strong Indian (Assam recommended) and carefully filtered to remove any leaves.

10. Short Glossary of Drinking Terms

By using the index, many facts on a wide variety of drink-related matters may be discovered. However, we deem it of value to collate short definitions of some common terms. We have not confined ourselves to matters relevant to mixed drinks. For convenience of reference, we repeat, in concise form, information on certain subjects dealt with elsewhere.

To some readers, this selection – necessarily a personal one – may appear to include rather obvious topics. But what is commonplace to one person may be unfamiliar to another. There is no pretension that this is a comprehensive list: it is designed to cover a sensible number of words and phrases with which people may be confronted during travels, or conversationally.

A

Abboccato Italian description of medium-sweet wine.

Abocado Spanish equivalent to above.

Adega Portuguese wine store.

Advocaat Sweetened egg yolks blended with brandy and herbs. Though copied elsewhere, essentially a product of the Netherlands.

Aguardiente Generic term in Spanish-speaking countries for distilled spirits.

Alcool Blanc Colourless, unmatured French distillation, particularly fruit brandy.

Amontillado Commonest and most popular of Spanish sherries for export: medium dry. Good for most mixed drinks.

Amoroso Sherry term not employed in Spain. It describes a sherry sweetened for the British market, where it is less popular than formerly.

Angelica Very sweet liqueur from French Basque country. Also: a form of Californian white 'port', a mixture of brandy and partly fermented grape juice, said to have taken its name from Los Angeles in the days of the Catholic missions.

Applejack The American equivalent of Calvados. Originally this was made during New England winters

145

by exposing casks of cider so the water froze, leaving behind a high proportion of alcohol, if a somewhat impure one.

Aqua vitae 'Water of life': the ancient Latin words for alcohol, particularly applied to spirits. From *aqua vitae* derive *Aquavit, akavit, usquebaugh* (whisky), *eau de vie, wodka*, etc.

Arrack Also Arak, Raki, etc. Terms used for various distillations from East Europe to Indonesia. The best was once considered that made from fermented palm-tree sap (toddy) but associated spirits come from many bases, including dates, grape juice, rice, milk, and sugar cane.

Thus flavour is much a question of local taste. The name comes from an Arabic word for 'juice' (or 'perspiration').

Asciutto Generic Italian term for dry wine.

Auslese German term for wine made from selected bunches of grapes: too good for mixed drinks.

B

Ballon French balloon-shaped glass, of various sizes, for concentrating aroma of fine brandy.

Bantu Beer Also called Kaffir Beer; South African brew from various grains enjoying benefit of low taxation.

Barrique French barrel (hogshead) varying marginally in different districts. Best known is the Bordeaux barrel with capacity of 225 litres, notionally equivalent to 288 bottles of wine.

Beerenauslese Superior German white wine made from selected grapes.

Bianco Italian term to describe white wine; particularly associated with pale, sweet vermouth.

Blanc White (French).

Blanc de blancs White wine made entirely from white grapes, especially champagne.

Blanc de noirs White wine made from red grapes; a term not much used outside wine-making circles.

Bond English term for store under governmental controls where taxable products (notably alcohol) may be kept without paying duty, which is only paid when they are finally withdrawn for sale in normal UK trade.

Booze see Chapter 9.

Bothan Illegal Scottish drinking-den.

Botanicals Herbal ingredients for flavouring gin, liqueurs, bitters, etc.

Bouchon Cork (French).

Bouchonné 'Corked' wine: wine infected by a diseased cork.

Boukha Form of brandy distilled in North Africa, mainly Tunisia, and usually based on figs.

Bouquet The internationally-employed French word for the indefiniable aroma that emanates from good wine, also from fine spirits.

Brännvin Another word for aquavit, particularly in Norway.

Brut Describes very dry champagne. It is now also applied to other dry sparkling wines of less distinction.

C

Cane spirit Distillation from molasses, the residual element in cane sugar production. Cane spirit is the basis of much rum. Highly rectified in continuous (patent) stills, at best cane spirit is an extremely pure spirit and is the basis of many good gins, aquavits, and unflavoured vodkas.

Caramel Burnt sugar widely used to give colour to beverages, and particularly evident in standardising the colour of blended whiskies. So little is needed to add coloration even to dark rum, that the taste of the product is quite unaffected.

Carbonation The process of adding carbon dioxide (CO_2), *gaz carbonique*, to wines and other beverages to give them artificial sparkle. CO_2 is produced naturally during fermentation: its most celebrated straightforward use is in the costly champagne process.

Cassis Blackcurrant syrup. Mildly alcoholic *crème de cassis*, the best coming from the Dijon area of France, is the basis for Kir.

Cava Spanish equivalent of méthode Champenoise.

Chai Above-ground French cellar in Bordeaux region and Cognac.

Chambrer Widely-used French verb to describe naturally bringing a wine to the temperature of the room in which it is to be served. Red wines are normally drunk *chambré*, though in this age of often excessive central-heating this may be too warm.

Cirrhosis Progressive, eventually fatal, liver complaint associated with heavy drinking and endemic in some wine-growing regions. But there are many other factors that induce or aggravate the disease, and many who imbibe much alcohol do not suffer from it.

Coffey Still Another name for the patent or continuous still, named after the man who perfected it.

Combustion 'Spontaneous combustion', by which heavy drinkers burst into flames, was a myth relished by early temperance fanatics. Despite numerous alarming 'eye-witness' accounts, this phenomenon is unknown to science.

Congenerics or Congeners. Elements, other than potable alcohol, found in spirits. They may be harmful, to be removed by maturing or rectification, or essential natural flavour as in whisky.

Corked see *Bouchonné*

Crackling American term to describe slightly sparkling wines.

Crème Very sweet alcoholic cordial: a huge variety exists.

Crust English term for deposit thrown by wine long stored in bottle, particularly port.

Cuve French wine vat.

Cuvée Wine from the contents of a single vat (France). The word has special reference to wine that is to be made into champagne. But terms like 'special cuvée' should be treated with reserve unless allied to a well-known name.

Cuve close System employed to produce sparkling wine in bulk, as opposed to the Champagne method. It can produce quality wines and must not be confused with artificial carbonisation.

D

De luxe This French term denoting high quality is carried by many fine brands, particularly spirits, but has no legal definition and is only meaningful when associated with names of repute.

Demijohn A corruption of the French *Dame-Jeanne*: a large glass flagon such as is used to preserve very special Cognac

147

which has achieved maximum cask-age. Also a particular Bordeaux bottle with 2½ litres capacity.

Demi-sec Literally 'semi-dry', but the term is particularly used in connection with Champagne, when it means 'fairly sweet'.

Dop South African brandy of the *marc* type.

Draff Solid residue left after fermentation of barley in whisky production: a valuable food for livestock.

Dry This English word has become internationalised as meaning un-sweetened. It is applied mainly to wines, including fortified varieties. In spirits its main application is to gin.

E

Eau de vie widely employed French term for spirits, which range from finest brandy to distillations better described as *eau de mort.*

Espumoso Sparkling (Spanish).

F

Feints Unpleasing spirit – 'tops and tails' – at the beginning and end of a single pot-still distillation, especially Scotch whisky. Feints are eliminated from the final product.

Fiasco Wine bottle of flask shape, particularly associated with the straw-covered Chianti bottle. Use of the word in

many languages to describe failure may derive from the fact that an empty bottle is a disaster or from use of *fiasco* by Venetian glassblowers to describe bad workmanship.

Fine Champagne A semantic trap for the uninitiated: it is a blend of Cognac from the two most prestigious areas and absolutely nothing to do with Champagne as a wine. In France, colloquially '*une fine*' is a way of ordering a simple brandy by the glass.

Fining Process of clarifying beverages, by introduction of a wide range of materials.

Fino Driest style of sherry.

Firkin Small, 9-gallon (40.5 litres) British wine barrel.

Fluid Ounce Basic measure widely used in English-speaking countries, particularly for service of spirits. Imperial fluid ounce is 2.84 cl and the American is marginally larger at 2.95 cl.

Foreshots First rough feints (see above).

Frappé Drink served with

crushed ice: e.g. *crème de menthe frappé.*

Fusel Oil Displeasing, even noxious, alcohols and some other (congeneric) elements existing in varying amounts in newly distilled spirits. They may be removed by maturing, re-distilling or rectification.

G

Gallon British (Imperial) equals 4.54 litres. U.S. Gallon is the old British 'wine (or bulk) gallon', superseded in 1826. The U.S. gallon is equivalent to 3.78 litres. Thus the U.S. gallon is virtually ⅚th of a British gallon.

Gauger Scottish term for an excise officer: one who registers (gauges) the strength of alcohol for tax purposes.

Gill Quarter of a pint. One-sixth of a gill is the usual official spirit measure – '6-out' – of English public houses and hotel bars. We prefer the more generous 1 fl. oz/25 ml.

Glacé A drink served very cold by refrigeration or use of ice cubes ('on the rocks') but not

quite the same as *frappé* (q.v.).
Gomme French sugar syrup.
Grain Spirit Distillation from cereals, as opposed to Cane spirit (q.v.).
Grain whisky Though all Scotch whisky is distilled from cereal, this term is used to describe whisky made in Scotland from (mainly) maize and some barley by patent distillation, for blending with Scotch malt whisky (wholly from barley) distilled in pot-stills.
Grappa Italian equivalent of *marc*; distillation from wine residue.
Grenadine Syrup much used in cocktails, traditionally pomegranate-flavoured.

H

Hectare For the non-metricated, this is 2.47 acres (10,000 square metres).
Hectolitre 100 litres: 21.99 British (Imperial) gallons, 26.41 American gallons.
Hock An English word for what used to be called 'Rhenish'; not a term used by Rhine wine-makers.
Hollands Slightly old-fashioned name for Dutch gin (Geneva, Genever, Schiedam).

J

Jigger American, and by adoption, British term for measure (about 1 fl. oz) of spirits.

K

Kaffir beer See Bantu beer.
Kir Canon Kir died in 1968, aged 92. He was a noted cleric, member of the French parliament and long-time Major of Dijon, and bestowed his name (q.v.) on a famous drink: Chapter 9.

Korn (Brantwein) Spirit from cereals, often rye, distilled principally in Germany; it may be variously flavoured.
Koumiss Caucasian drink made from fermented milk – mare's, cow's, and sometimes camel's. Also known in Siberia; similar beverages are called Kafir (Kefir).
Kvass Eastern European and Russian brew, made at home, from fermented cereals and bread, with fruit or sugar to sweeten.

L

Liquor Whilst the English-language colloquial meaning is

strong alcohol, in distilling and brewing liquor means water.
Low wines First, low strength, distillation of whisky from which the final product is re-distilled.

M

Malt Sprouting cereal, principally barley, which has been dried: see Scotch whisky.
Marc *eau de vie de marc:* French spirit distilled from residue after grape pressing (*pomace*).
Mead Fermented honey alcoholic beverage of immense antiquity and once in very widespread use. Name is thought to come from old Sanskrit *madhu* (honey).
Méthode Champenoise Method of making sparkling wine entirely naturally in the bottle, without any artificial carbonisation – as used for Champagne.
Mistelle Unfermented grape juice to which spirit has been added, producing a sweet, cheap drink which does not reserve the name wine. Pineau is a superior form.
Moonshine American term for illicitly distilled spirit, indicating that it is probably made at night to lower chances of detection. The word is also applied colloquially to legal but poor quality whiskey.
Mousseux French description for all sparkling wines, except Champagne: it covers a wide range of qualities.
Mull English word for warming

149

and spicing, and often fortifying, wine or beer.

Neutral spirit Anglo-American term for unflavoured strong alcohol. Also known, particularly in Scotland, as silent spirit.

Ojen Spanish generic term for absinthe-style beverages.
Orgeat Almond-flavoured alcohol fairly well-known in the U.S.A.
Ouzo Very popular Greek spirit of *pastis* style.

Passion fruit The delicious juice of this fruit is too much neglected by devotees of mixed drinks.
Pastis French aniseed-flavoured alcohols which replaced absinthe.
Patent Still For continuous distillation, as opposed to pot-still; also called Coffey still.
Perry Similar to cider but made from pears; less common than formerly.
Pétillant French wine that is slightly sparkling by natural processes, not carbonated.
Pisco General South American distillation from wine, the best from Peru.
Plonk See Chapter 9.
Pomace Residue after pressing of grapes or fruit. Pomace Brandy is Californian

equivalent of *marc* or *grappa*.
Pot Still Original style.
Poteen (Potheen) 'Pochen': illegal Irish whiskey.
Premium Rather meaningless colloquial term to denote above-average quality, we hope, and certainly above-average cost.

Quetsch Alsace-Lorraine version of plum brandy, similar to *slivovitz* but customarily superior.
Quinine Botanical ingredient much used to add bitter character to proprietary brands of aperitifs. It comes from chichona bark and enjoys a medicinal reputation (it was the first specific against malaria). Indian Quinine Water was the origin of 'tonic' water.

R

Raki Balkan term for Arrack, etc.; spirit from no particular source nor of any distinction.

Ratafia Antique term covering any liqueur, usually made at home; produced by fortifying wine with brandy, fruit flavourings and sweeteners and allowing mixture to improve in bottle.
Rectification By re-distilling to remove impurities from spirit.
Ron Rum (Spanish).
Rosato Italian for *rosé* wine.
Rosé Generic term for French 'pink' wines, now employed almost internationally.

S

Samogon Russian equivalent of 'moonshine' or poteen.

Schiedam Originally, and still, the home of Dutch gin; the town's name was once a synonym for the product.
Schnapps Many and variously flavoured spirits in Germany and the Netherlands meaning much the same as Aquavit.
Sec French for 'dry'.
Secco Italian for *sec*.
Sekt Sparkling wine (German).
Shebeen Irish illicit drinking den.

Shrub English mixed drink popular in 18th century; composed of rum or brandy usually, with spices, herbs, sweetening, juices. A form of it has been revived commercially in the West Country.

Sommelier Originally the factotum in a great French *château* who had charge of linen, plate and provisions, particularly the wine-cellar. The term now means a wine-butler or principal wine-waiter in a restaurant.

Specific gravity Weight of an alcoholic liquid as against that of equal amount of water: mainly used in measuring potency of beer.

Spritzig German for slightly sparkling wine.

Spumante Sparkling (Italian).

Strega Generic term for a sweet, traditional Italian liqueur.

Swizzle-stick Colloquial name for an instrument to remove effervescence from a beverage; sometimes made in

expensive metals for plutocrats to eliminate an essential aspect of rare Champagne. Technically known as a *mosser*.

T

Tastevin Traditional, still employed, shallow silver cup used by wine-tasters, especially in Burgundy: its polished surface reflects clarity of a wine. The tastevin has also become a ceremonial feature associated with *sommeliers*.

Trester German equivalent of *marc* (q.v.).

Triple sec Now a generic term for white *curaçao*.

Trocken Dry (German).

U

Usquebaugh Celtic translation of *aqua vitae* – also *uisge beatha usky, wusky* . . . hence whisk(e)y.

V

Vatting Blending; particularly in connection with Scotch Whisky.

Vinegar *vinaigre* (sour wine); at its simplest highly oxidized wine, but in effect much more complicated for fine vinegars with special flavourings; also made from cider, malt, etc.

V.S.O.P. 'Very Special (or Superior) Old Pale'; designation for good grade of Cognac; see main text for fuller explanation.

W

Wash Type of 'beer', from fermentation of wort, from which whisky is distilled.

Weeper British term for bottle or cask leaking through defective cork or timber.

Whisky/Whiskey The convention of the two spellings is of quite recent origin.

Wort Sweet extract from malt from which the wash (q.v.) is made. See Whisky in main text.

X

Xeres French official description of Sherry – *vin de Jerez* ('hereth'); Xeres was old Roman name for the town.

X.O. Extra Old – but indicates no precise age.

Z

Zubrowka Vodka from Poland (and Russia) lightly flavoured with special wild grass.

D.I.Y.

Personal Cocktails

Title _____

Ingredients & quantities: _____

_____

_____

_____

Method: _____

_____

_____

_____

Garnish/Decoration: _____

_____

Origin: _____

Date: _____

Comments: _____

_____

Title _____

Ingredients & quantities _____

_____

_____

_____

Method: _____

_____

_____

_____

Garnish/Decoration: _____

_____

Origin; _____

Date: _____

Comments: _____

Plese send in any queries concerning drink related matters (along with s.a.e.) to: Peter Dominic Wine Mine Club, Vintner House, River Way, Harlow, Essex.

Title _____

Ingredients and quantities: _____

_____

_____

_____

Method: _____

_____

_____

_____

Garnish/Decoration: _____

_____

Origin: _____

Date: _____

Comments: _____

Title _____

Ingredients and quantities: _____

_____

_____

_____

Method: _____

_____

_____

_____

Garnish/Decoration: _____

_____

Origin: _____

Date: _____

Comments: _____

Title _____

Ingredients and quantities: _____

_____

_____

_____

Method: _____

_____

_____

_____

Garnish/Decoration: _____

_____

Origin: _____

Date: _____

Comments: _____

Title _____

Ingredients and quantities: _____

_____

_____

_____

Method: _____

_____

_____

_____

Garnish/Decoration: _____

_____

Origin: _____

Date: _____

Comments: _____

Title _____

Ingredients & quantities: _____

_____

_____

_____

Method: _____

_____

_____

_____

Garnish/Decoration: _____

_____

Origin: _____

Date: _____

Comments: _____

Title _____

Ingredients and quantities: _____

_____

_____

_____

Method: _____

_____

_____

_____

Garnish/Decoration: _____

_____

Origin: _____

Date: _____

Comments: _____

Title _____

Ingredients & quantities _____

_____

_____

_____

Method: _____

_____

_____

_____

Garnish/Decoration: _____

_____

Origin; _____

Date: _____

Comments: _____

Title _____

Ingredients and quantities: _____

_____

_____

_____

Method: _____

_____

_____

_____

Garnish/Decoration: _____

_____

Origin: _____

Date: _____

Comments: _____

Title _____
Ingredients and quantities: _____

_____
_____
_____

Method: _____
_____
_____
_____

Garnish/Decoration: _____

Origin: _____
Date: _____
Comments: _____

Title _____
Ingredients and quantities: _____

_____
_____
_____

Method: _____
_____
_____
_____

Garnish/Decoration: _____

Origin: _____
Date: _____
Comments: _____

Title _____
Ingredients and quantities: _____

_____
_____
_____

Method: _____
_____
_____
_____

Garnish/Decoration: _____

Origin: _____
Date: _____
Comments: _____

Title _____
Ingredients and quantities: _____

_____
_____
_____

Method: _____
_____
_____
_____

Garnish/Decoration: _____

Origin: _____
Date: _____
Comments: _____

Peter Dominic

In 1939 Paul Dauthieu opened his first wine shop in Horsham, Sussex. Feeling his own name to be unpronounceable he decided to trade under the more memorable title of Peter Dominic. On joining the RAF in 1940 he left the business in the hands of his wife, Blanche, and on his return in 1944 discovered she had run the business so successfully that she had had to increase her staff to 11 people. By 1963 when Paul decided to sell the company to International Distillers and Vintners he had 21 shops.

From most modest beginnings in 1939 Peter Dominic has grown to become the leading high street Wine Merchants of the present day, the 460 branches nationwide providing an impressive choice with around 400 wines and numerous spirits and liqueurs listed.

The customer can also make use of the many services offered by the company, for example the Party Service comprising free delivery on a minimum order of £25.00, goods on a sale or return basis and loan of glasses. There are also monthly promotions of selected wines and spirits and a wide range of Party Sundries including the William Levene 'Cocktail Makers' range as illustrated earlier in this book. Credit card facilities for the major credit card companies are also available including the Peter Dominic/Grand Metropolitan credit card also acceptable in many hotels and restaurants under the umbrella of Grand Metropolitan. However, without doubt, the most important service offered by Peter Dominic, is the expert and friendly advice of its staff, backed up by the wine expertise of its central management.

We are sure that, with the expert and friendly guidance given by John Doxat in this book, you will enjoy reviving that bygone Cocktail era of the roaring '20s.

Acknowledgements

Peter Dominic would like to thank the following

Graeme Harris
Peter Brennan
Harrods
The Cocktail Shop
IDV UK Ltd
W & A Gilbey Ltd
Bombay Spirits Company Ltd
Hatch Mansfield
Saccone and Speed
House of Seagram
J R Parkington
Rutherford Osborne and
    Perkin Ltd
House and Garden
The Mary Evans Picture
    Library
William Levene Limited
Pictor International – London

Cover photograph by courtesy of Vogue Promotions.

Index

A

Abbey, 84
Absinthe, 28
Absinthe Special, 120
Acapulco (i), 97
Acapulco (ii), 130
Ace, 116
Adam and Eve, 135
Addison, 84
Admiral, 104
Admiral's Highball, 104
Adonis, 129
advanced recipes, 135–40
Advocaat, 52, 61
Affinity, 102
Agony, 84
akavit, 30
Alaska, 84
alcohol, 12, 14–15, 18, 30–1
alcohols, white, 30–1
alcools blancs, 30–1
Ale Flip, 125
Alexandra, 116
Alonquin, 105
Amaretto di Saronno, 52
Ambassadeur, 51
Americano, 129
American whiskey, 35–7
Amer Picon, 50
Amontillado sherry, 61
Angel's Lips, 116
Anglo-American vodka, 22
Angostura, 62, 141
Anis, 52
Anisette, 52
Antonio, 109
Aperitifs, 49–52, 61
Apollinaris, 65
Apollo, 116
Apple, 120
Applejack, 44
Applejack Rabbit, 120
apple juice, 64
aquavit, 30
aqua vitae, 14
Armagnac, 42
Arrack, 28
Atholl Brose (i), 102

Atholl Brose (ii), 142
Australia, 38, 144
Australian whisky, 38

B

B and B, 143
Bacardi Cocktail, 97
Baccio Punch, 123
Bailey's, 10, 54, 55, 61
Balalaika, 93
Baltimore, 116
Bamboo, 129
Banana Cow, 116
Barbara West, 85
Barbra, 116
Barney Barnato, 109
beer, 60
Bees Knees, 85
Benedict Arnold, 102
Bénédictine, 54, 61, 143
Benny, 109
Bentley, 120
Betsy Ross, 109
Betty James, 85
Between the Sheets, 109
Bianco, 48
Bishop, 129
Bishop, English, 136
Bitter Lemon, 64
Bitters, 50, 62–3
blackcurrant syrup, 63
Blackrussian, 93
Black Stripe, 126
Black Velvet, 142
Blimlet, 135
Blood and Sand, 102
Bloody Maria, 99
Bloody Mary, 23, 94
Bloody Virgin, 130
Blue Bird, 85
Blue Bols, 58
Blue Lagoon, 93
Bobby Burns, 102
Bogus Colonel, 91
Boilermaker, 105
Bolero, 113
Bombay, 109
Bonanza, 109
Bonnie Prince Charlie, 109
Booster, 110

booze, 144
Boston Club, 85
Boston Cooler, 97
Bourbon, 35–7
Bourbon Fog, 123
Brain Buster, 69
Brainstorm, 105
Branca *fernet*, 51, 62–3
brandy, 12, 14, 15, 18, 22, 30–1, 34, 39–42, 44
Brandy Alexander, 110, 117
brandy-based recipes, 109–13
Brandy Cassis, 110
Brandy Flip, 117
Brandy Tot, 126
Brandy Zoom, 117
Britain, 14, 21–5, 28, 30, 39, 41, 42, 44, 45, 59, 61, 62, 63, 68, 143, 144
Bristol, 22
Broadmoor, 114
Bronx, 85
Brooklyn, 105
Buckaroo, 105
Buck's Fizz, 142
Bulldog, 85
Bulldog Highball, 120
Bullshot, 94
Bumble Bee, 110
Bunny Hug, 105
Bushmill's Black, 37
Buster, 114
Byrrh, 51

C

Cafe Italiano, 117
Cafe Royal, 136
California, 23, 38
calvados, 44–5
Campari, 50, 61
Canadian Cherry, 105
Canadian whisky, 31, 37
capacity measures, 81, 84
Capetown, 105
Capucine, 130–1

Caribbean, 24
Caribbean Dawn, 136
Caribbean Swizzle, 126
Carpano, 50
Casino de Paris, 137
Cayenne pepper, 64
Chambéry, 49
Champagne, 61, 142
Champagne Cocktail, 137
Charley Goodleg, 99
Chartreuse, 54–5, 61
Chatterley, Lady, 85
Cheers, 105
cherries, cocktail, 64
Cherry Blossom, 110
Cherry Brandy, 31, 45, 59, 61
Cherry Heering, 59–60
Cherry Rum, 117
Chicago (i), 110
Chicago (ii), 120
China, 14, 31
Churchill, 102
cider, 60, 61
Cider Cooler, 129
Cider Cup, 123
Cinderella, 130
cinnamon sticks, 65
Claret Cup, 123
Claret Refresher, 129
Cloak and Dagger, 114
Clover Club, 85
cocktails, origin of, 10, 66–71
cocktail cherries, 64
cocktail shakers, 72
Coco-gin, 87
Coconutty, 114
Cocoteq, 99
Coffey, Aeneas, 15
Coffey still, 15, 33
Cognac, 15, 39–41, 59, 143
Cointreau, 55, 61
Cola, 64
Collins, 87
Connoisseur, 117
Co-op, 120
Corpse Reviver, 133
cream-based recipes, 116–20

Cream Puff, 118
Crème de Cacao, 55
Crème de Cassis, 55, 63
Crème de Menthe, 55, 61
Crèmes, 55
Cuba Libre, 98
Cuban rum, 24
Curaçao, 55, 58
Cymraeg Chwisgi, 38
Cyprus, 42, 61

D

Dallas, 106
dark rum, 12, 15, 43–4, 66
dark rum-based recipes, 113–16
Demerara rum, 24
Depth Charge, 87
Devil's Own, 129
Diabolo, 129
Diaquiri, 98
Dinner-Time, 118
Dirty Dog, 110
distillation, 12, 14–15
distillation, continuous, 15, 18
Dizzy, 106
Don't Go Near the Water, 110
Dog's Hair, 133
Drambuie, 58, 61, 142
Dream, 110
Dry Martini, 48, 87, 88
Dry Vermouth, 48
Dublin, 15
Dubonnet, 50–1, 61
Dubonny, 87
Dunlop, 114
Dutch gin, 21

E

Earthquake, 88
eau de vie, 14, 31
Egg Nog, 120
El Diablo, 99
El Presidente, 114
Emerald Isle, 88

England, 15, 21–2, 33–4, 60, 69
English Bishop, 136
Epee, 110
equipment, 72–8
Erotica, 137
Europe, 14, 28, 31
Exorcist, 99

F

fermentation, 12
Fernet (Branca), 51, 62–3
Fibber McGee, 88
Fifth Avenue, 118
Finland, 22
First Aid, 131
Fish House Punch, 139
Florida, 88
Fluffy Duck, 88
Flying Scotsman, 102
France, 14, 39–42, 44, 46, 48–9, 50, 51, 54, 59, 61, 142
Freddy Fudpucker, 100
French brandy, 22, 39–42
French Kiss, 88
'fruit brandies', 30–1, 45
Fun in Bed, 106

G

Galliano, 58–9
G and T, 120–1
garnishes, 80
Gentle John, 102
Georgia Beauty, 110
Germany, 30, 42, 61, 63
Gibson, 88, 89
Gilbey's, 21, 24
Gimlet, 88–9
gin, 15, 18–22, 30, 65, 66, 141, 143
Gin and Ginger, 120
gin-based recipes, 84–92
Gin Fizz, 89
Gin Rickey, 89

Ginger Ale, 64
glasses, 76–7, 81, 83
glasses, mixing, 73–4
Glayra, 59
Gloom-lifter, 106
Glühwein, 126
Godfather, 107
Gold Coconut, 110
Golden Cadillac, 118
Gold Fizzer, 90
Granada, 111
Grand Marnier, 59
grape juice, 64
Green-Eyed Monster, 107
green olives, 65
Grenadier, 111
Grenadine, 63
grapefruit juice, 64
Grigio Verde, 121
Grog, 128
Guinness, 142
Gunga Din, 90

H

Hangover, 69
Hari-Kari, 107
Harry Lauder, 102
Harvey Wallbanger, 97
Havana, 98
Havana Beach, 99
Headless Horseman, 97
Heart Starter, 133
Hell, 111
Hennessy, Richard, 42
Heublein's, 22–3
Highball, 105
Hole-in-One, 103
Hollywood, 99
Horse's Neck, 111
hot drinks, 126–8
hot punches, 125–6
Hungary, 31

I

ice, 65, 77–8, 80–1, 82
Income Tax, 90
India, 14, 144

Ireland, 37
Irish coffee, 142
Irish Mist, 59
Irish Velvet, 59
Irish whiskey, 34, 37, 54, 59, 142
Italy, 42, 46–7, 51, 52, 58, 60, 61
Itchy Bitchy, 111

J

Jamaica, 60
Jamaican Glory, 116
Jamaican rum, 24
Japan, 14, 37, 144
Japanese whisky, 37–8
Jelly Beans, 69
Jerez, 129
John Collins, 90
John's Bowl, 123
juices, 63–4

K

Kahlua, 59
Kir, 51, 142
Kirsch, 31
Kiss Me Quick, 121
Kiss the Boys Goodbye, 111
Kitty Love, 121
Klondyke, 129
Knickerbocker, 90
Knockout, 139
Kornbrandtweins, 30
Kümmel, 59

L

Lady Chatterley, 85
Last Resort, 112
lemonade, 64
lemon juice, 63
lemons, 64
Liberal, 107
Lichee, 139
Lillet, 51

lime juice, 63
lime juice cordial, 63
Limey, 131
liqueurs, 18, 52, 54–5, 58–60, 61
Loch Lomond, 103
London Dry gin, 19, 21, 22
Londoner, 90
London Fog, 90
Long Boat, 131
Los Angeles, 107
Louisiana, 139

M

Macho, 100
Maiden's Prayer, 90
Mai Tai, 116
Malibu, 10, 51–2. 59, 61
Malibu Iceberg, 118
Malvern water, 65
Mandarine, 59
Manhattan, 107, 108
Maraschino, 59
marc de Bourgogne, 42
Margarita, 25, 101, 102
Marlborough, 97
Marseilles, 28
Martin, John, 22–3
Martinez, 90–1
Martini, 48, 87, 88
Mary Pickford, 99
Mead, 143
measures, 76, 81, 84
Mexico, 25, 28, 59
Mexican Rose, 101
Mickey Finn, 91
Mint Julep, 108, 109
Minty, 131
Moscow Mule, 23, 97
Muscovital, 97

N

Napoleon brandy, 41, 42
Navy rum, 43
Negroni, 91
Negus, 67

Netherlands, 21, 38, 39, 59
New Zealand, 38
New Yorker, 91
Nogg, 126, 128
non-alcoholic drinks, 130–2
non-spirit cocktails, 129–32
nutmeg, 65

O

Ojen, 28
Old Fashioned, 108
Old Smoothe, 97
Old Tom gin, 21
olives, 65
onions, 64
Oporto, 129
orange bitters, 62
Orange Bloom, 91
orange juice, 64
oranges, 64
Ouzo, 28

P

Parfait Amour, 59
Parson's Particular, 131
party drinks, 122–5
passion fruit, 64
pastis, 28, 61
pearl onions, 64
Peppermint cordial, 63
Pernod, 28, 30, 61, 78
Perrier, 65
Peter Herring's, 59–60
Peter's Grasshopper, 118
Piccadilly, 91
Pick-Me-Up, 63, 133
Pimms, 91
Pimms Royale, 139
Pimms Special, 139
Pina Colada, 99
pineapple juice, 64
Pineau, 51
Pink gin, 21, 141
Pink Lady, 118

Planter's Punch (i), 116
Planter's Punch (ii), 139
Platinum Blonde, 118
Playboy, 121
plonk, 144
Plymouth gin, 21, 22, 141
Poire Williams, 31
Poland, 22
Polish vodka, 22
Port, 61
Port Flip (i), 118
Port Flip (ii), 130
Port Negus, 128
Potheen, 37
Pousse cafe, 143–4
Prairie Oyster, 134
Prince Edward, 103
Prohibition, 69, 131
Puerto Rico, 24
punches, 44, 61, 64
punch recipes, 122–6, 139, 140
Punsch, 30
Punt e Mes, 50
Pussyfoot, 131

Q

Quebec, 108

R

Rabbit's Revenge, 108
recipe guide, 82–4
Red Vermouth, 47–8
Red Wine Mull, 126
Red Wine Punch, 123
restorative recipes, 133–4
Ricard, 28, 30
Rickey, 91
Robert Burns, 103
Rob Roy, 104
Rolls Royce, 91
Rose hip, 63
Rosé Vermouth, 49
Round the World, 121
Royal Mint Chocolate, 60

rum, dark, 12, 15, 43–4, 66
rum, white, 24–5
Rum Milk Punch, 118
Rum Moka, 118
Russian vodka, 22
Rusty Nail, 142–3
rye whiskey, 36

S

St Raphael, 51
Sake, 144
Sambuca, 60
Sangria, 143
Savoy Corpse-reviver, 133
Savoy Springbok, 121
Scarlett O'Hara, 121
Schiedam, Rotterdam, 21
Schnapps, 30
Scotch Solace, 119
Scotch whisky, 14, 15, 18, 31–8, 66, 143
Screwdriver, 23, 97
Serpent's Tooth, 108
shakers, 75, 79
Sheep Dip, 91
sherry, 61
Sherry Cobbler, 130
Sherry Punch, 125
Sidecar, 94, 112
Siegert, Dr J. G. B., 62
Silver Streak, 92
Singapore Gin Sling, 139
Slim Jim, 131
Slivovitz, 31
Sloe gin, 21, 143
Sloe Glow, 122
Sloppy Joe, 112
Smirnoff, 18, 22–3, 24
Smith and Wesson, 119
Snoopy, 108
Snifter, 112
Snowball, 122
soda-water, 64
Sour Mash, 37
South Africa, 60
South America, 24

Southern Comfort, 60, 61
Spain, 14, 38, 42, 143
Sparkling Punch, 125
spirit-based recipes, 120–2
spirits, general, 12, 13, 18, 30
spoons, bar, 74–5
Sportsman, 131
Spring Blossom, 122
squashes, 64
Starboard Light, 122
stills, 14–15
Stone Fence, 104
strainers, 73
Strega, 60
sugar syrup, 63
Sun, 112
Sunrise, 119
Sunset, 101
Suze, 51
Sweden, 22
Swedish Punsch, 60
Sweet and Sour, 122
Sym y Don, 38
syrups, 63

T

tabasco, 65
Tam O'Shanter, 128
Tea, 144
Tea Punch, 126
Temperance Tankard, 131
Temptation, 108
Tennessee, 108
tequila, 25–8, 81
tequila-based recipes, 99–102
Tequila Caliente, 102
Tequini, 102
Third Rail, 99
Three Star brandy, 40
Tia Maria, 60, 61
Tiger's Milk, 112
toasts, 144
Tom and Jerry, 140
tomato juice, 64
Tonga, 131

tonic water, 64
Trinity, 92
T.T., 132
Twister, 97

U

Underberg, 63
United Kingdom *see* Britain
USA, 8, 18, 22–3, 25, 28, 35–7, 44, 59, 60, 65, 67–9, 71, 134
usquebaugh, 14, 33

V

Van der Hum, 60
Velvet Gloves, 119
Vermouth, 46–9, 50, 61
Vermouth Cassis, 48, 130
Very Important Persons, 140
Viking, 122
vodka, 18, 22–4, 30, 66, 143
vodka-based recipes, 93–7
Vodkatini, 97
VSOP brandy, 40

W

Wales, 38
Washington Cooler, 125
water, 65
Weep No More, 113
West Indies, 15, 24
What's It?, 122
whiskey, 35–7
whiskey-based recipes, 104–8
whisky, 12, 14, 15, 18, 31–8, 66, 143
whisky-based recipes, 102–4

Whisky Mac, 143
Whisky Sour, 104
Whisky Toddy, 128
white alcohols, 30–1
White Elephant, 119
White Lady, 92, 94
White Mink, 119
white rum, 24–5. 30
white rum-based recipes, 97–9
white spirits, 18–31
White Wine Punch, 125
White Wine Zip, 130
wine, 60–1, 67, 142, 143, 144
Worcester Sauce, 64

Y

Yankee Invigorator, 133
Yellow Fever, 97
Yellow Lion, 132
Yes and No, 113
Yugoslavia, 59

Z

Zombie, 140